BATTLEFIELDS™

THE NIGHT WITCHES

VOLUME ONE

THE NIGHT WITCHES

Written by
GARTH ENNIS

Illustrated by
RUSS BRAUN

Colored by
TONY AVIÑA

Lettered by
SIMON BOWLAND

Collection and issue covers by
JOHN CASSADAY

Alternate #1 cover by
GARRY LEACH

"The Night Witches" logo designed by
JASON ULLMEYER

ENTERTAINMENT®

WWW.DYNAMITEENTERTAINMENT.COM

NICK BARRUCCI • PRESIDENT
JUAN COLLADO • CHIEF OPERATING OFFICER
JOSEPH RYBANDT • ASSOCIATE EDITOR
JOSH JOHNSON • CREATIVE DIRECTOR
JASON ULLMEYER • GRAPHIC DESIGNER

First Printing   ISBN-10: 1-60690-028-5   ISBN-13: 978-1-60690-028-4   10 9 8 7 6 5 4 3 2 1

CHAPTER 1

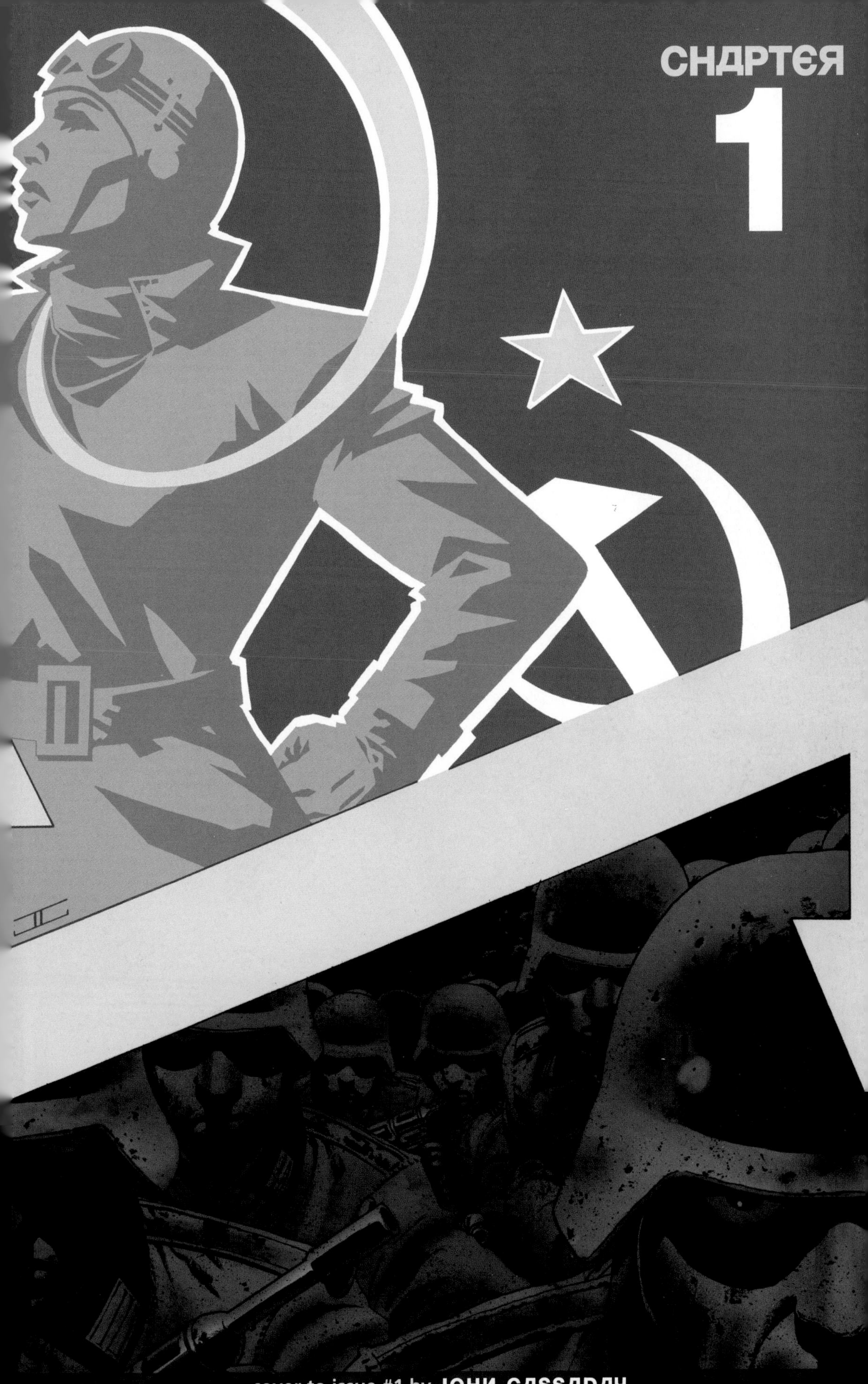

cover to issue #1 by **JOHN CASSADAY**

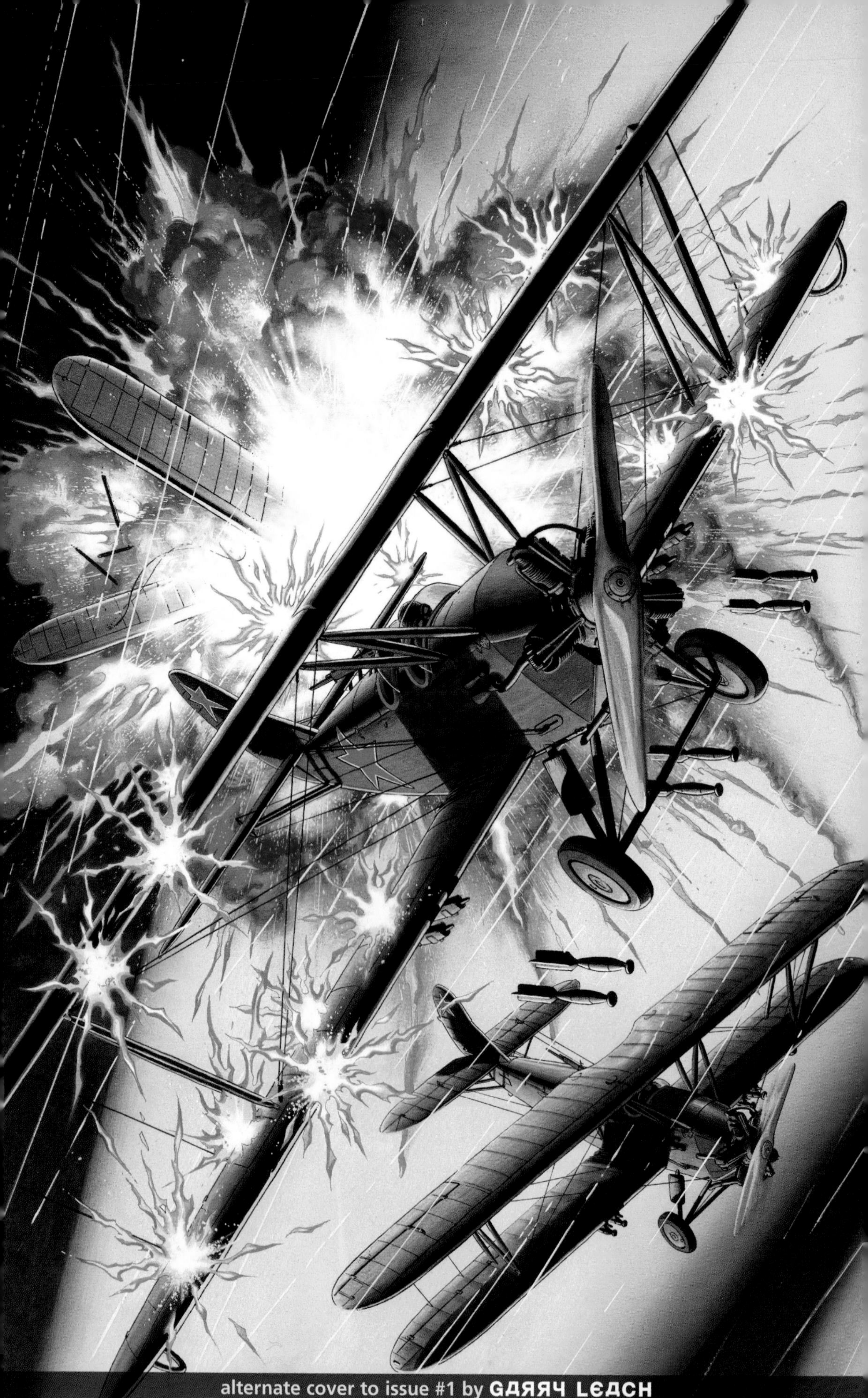

alternate cover to issue #1 by **GARRY LEACH**

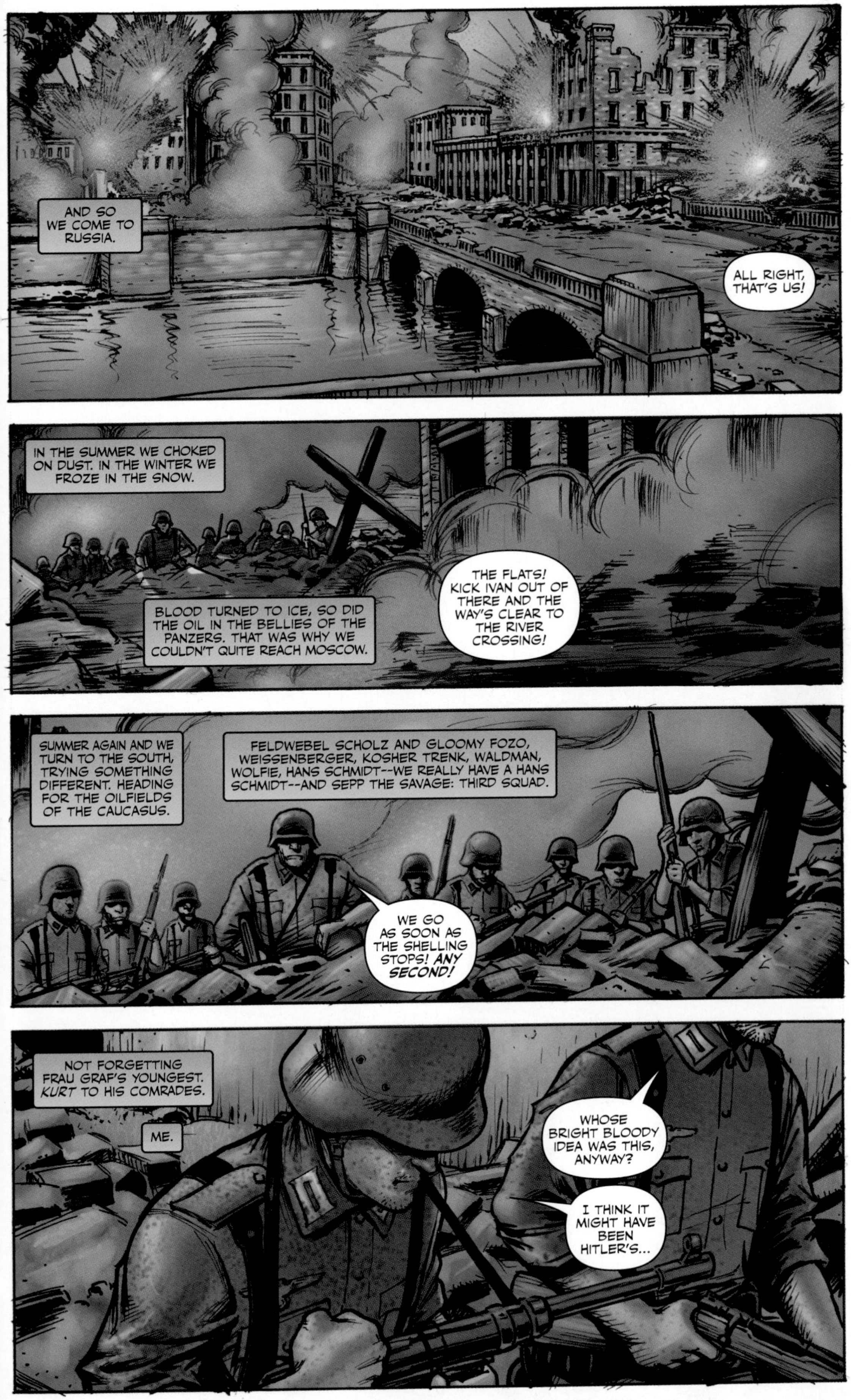
AND SO WE COME TO RUSSIA.
ALL RIGHT, THAT'S US!
IN THE SUMMER WE CHOKED ON DUST. IN THE WINTER WE FROZE IN THE SNOW.
BLOOD TURNED TO ICE, SO DID THE OIL IN THE BELLIES OF THE PANZERS. THAT WAS WHY WE COULDN'T QUITE REACH MOSCOW.
THE FLATS! KICK IVAN OUT OF THERE AND THE WAY'S CLEAR TO THE RIVER CROSSING!
SUMMER AGAIN AND WE TURN TO THE SOUTH, TRYING SOMETHING DIFFERENT. HEADING FOR THE OILFIELDS OF THE CAUCASUS.
FELDWEBEL SCHOLZ AND GLOOMY FOZO, WEISSENBERGER, KOSHER TRENK, WALDMAN, WOLFIE, HANS SCHMIDT--WE REALLY HAVE A HANS SCHMIDT--AND SEPP THE SAVAGE: THIRD SQUAD.
WE GO AS SOON AS THE SHELLING STOPS! *ANY SECOND!*
NOT FORGETTING FRAU GRAF'S YOUNGEST. *KURT* TO HIS COMRADES.
ME.
WHOSE BRIGHT BLOODY IDEA WAS THIS, ANYWAY?
I THINK IT MIGHT HAVE BEEN HITLER'S...

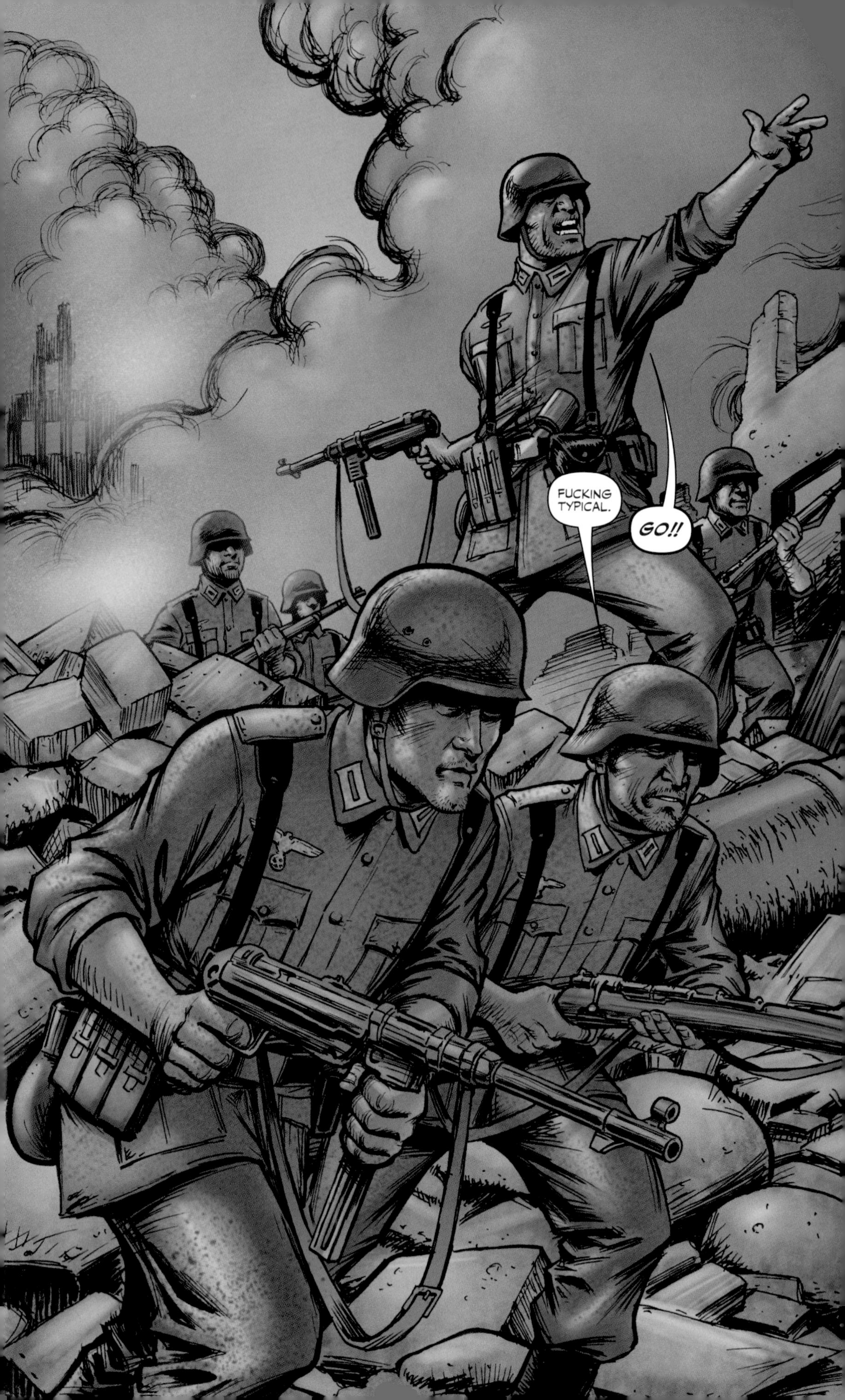
FUCKING TYPICAL.
GO!!

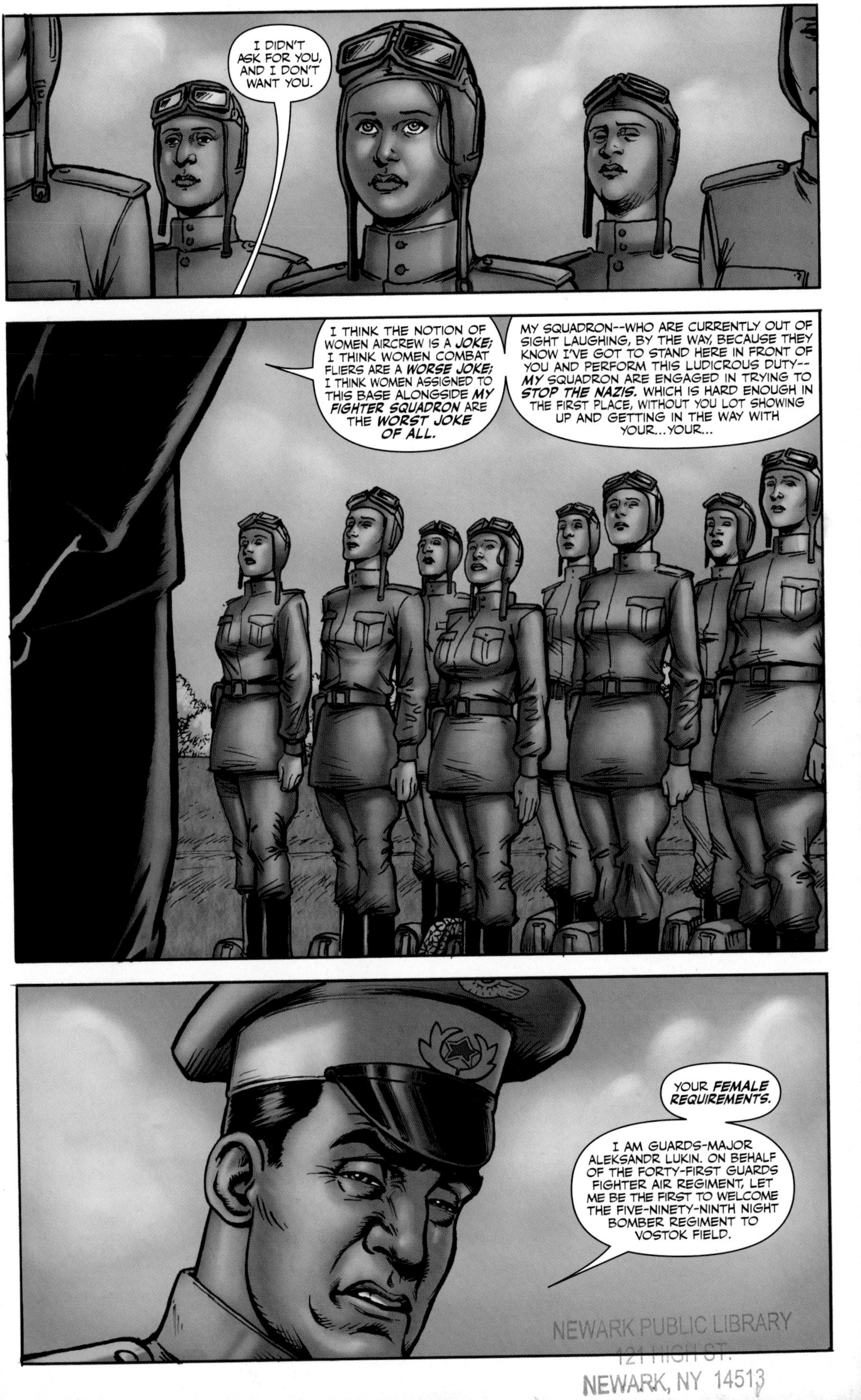
I DIDN'T ASK FOR YOU, AND I DON'T WANT YOU.
I THINK THE NOTION OF WOMEN AIRCREW IS A JOKE; I THINK WOMEN COMBAT FLIERS ARE A WORSE JOKE; I THINK WOMEN ASSIGNED TO THIS BASE ALONGSIDE MY FIGHTER SQUADRON ARE THE WORST JOKE OF ALL.
MY SQUADRON--WHO ARE CURRENTLY OUT OF SIGHT LAUGHING, BY THE WAY, BECAUSE THEY KNOW I'VE GOT TO STAND HERE IN FRONT OF YOU AND PERFORM THIS LUDICROUS DUTY--MY SQUADRON ARE ENGAGED IN TRYING TO STOP THE NAZIS. WHICH IS HARD ENOUGH IN THE FIRST PLACE, WITHOUT YOU LOT SHOWING UP AND GETTING IN THE WAY WITH YOUR...YOUR...
YOUR FEMALE REQUIREMENTS.
I AM GUARDS-MAJOR ALEKSANDR LUKIN. ON BEHALF OF THE FORTY-FIRST GUARDS FIGHTER AIR REGIMENT, LET ME BE THE FIRST TO WELCOME THE FIVE-NINETY-NINTH NIGHT BOMBER REGIMENT TO VOSTOK FIELD.

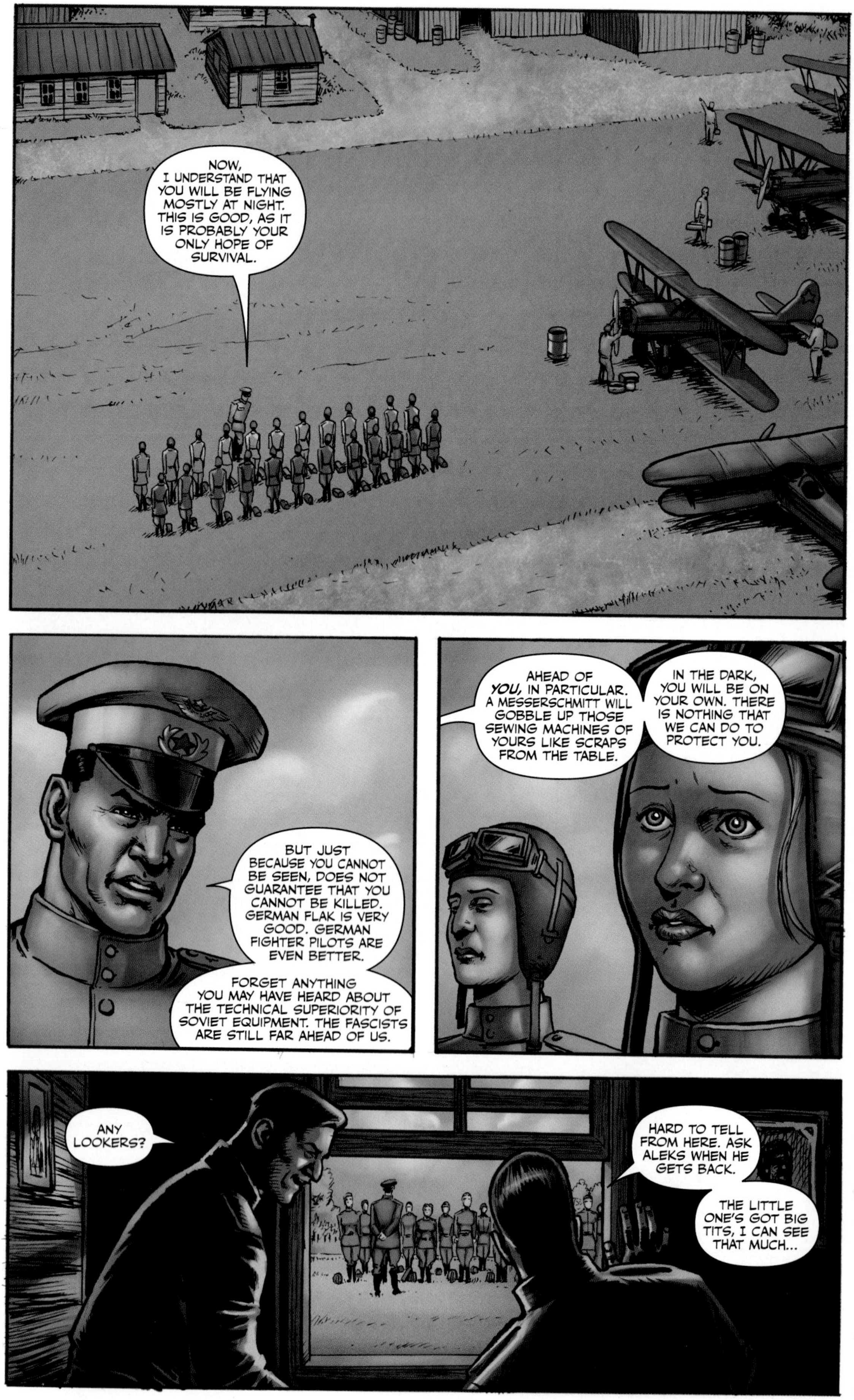
NOW, I UNDERSTAND THAT YOU WILL BE FLYING MOSTLY AT NIGHT. THIS IS GOOD, AS IT IS PROBABLY YOUR ONLY HOPE OF SURVIVAL.
BUT JUST BECAUSE YOU CANNOT BE SEEN, DOES NOT GUARANTEE THAT YOU CANNOT BE KILLED. GERMAN FLAK IS VERY GOOD. GERMAN FIGHTER PILOTS ARE EVEN BETTER.
FORGET ANYTHING YOU MAY HAVE HEARD ABOUT THE TECHNICAL SUPERIORITY OF SOVIET EQUIPMENT. THE FASCISTS ARE STILL FAR AHEAD OF US.
AHEAD OF *YOU,* IN PARTICULAR. A MESSERSCHMITT WILL GOBBLE UP THOSE SEWING MACHINES OF YOURS LIKE SCRAPS FROM THE TABLE.
IN THE DARK, YOU WILL BE ON YOUR OWN. THERE IS NOTHING THAT WE CAN DO TO PROTECT YOU.
ANY LOOKERS?
HARD TO TELL FROM HERE. ASK ALEKS WHEN HE GETS BACK.
THE LITTLE ONE'S GOT BIG TITS, I CAN SEE THAT MUCH...

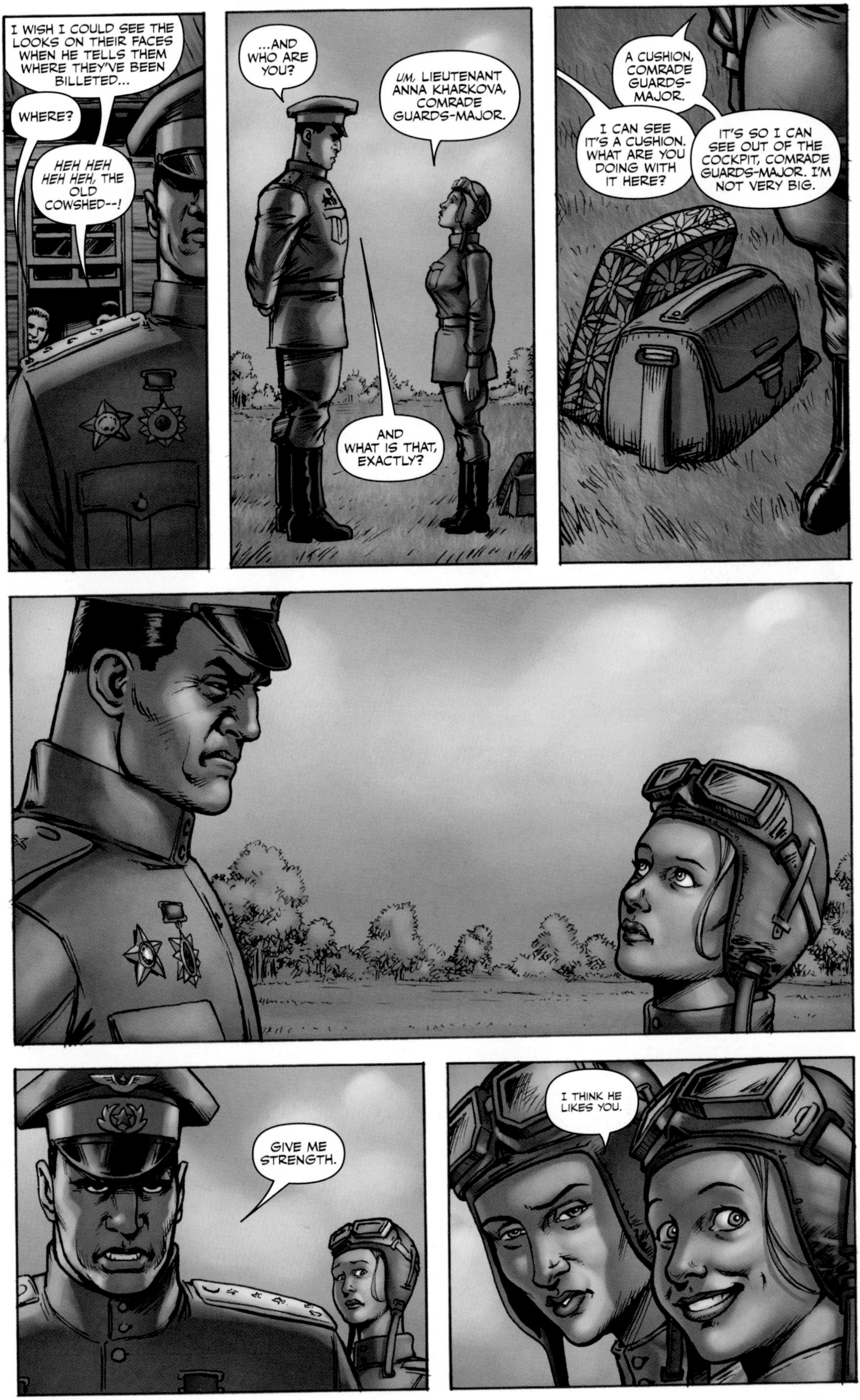

I WISH I COULD SEE THE LOOKS ON THEIR FACES WHEN HE TELLS THEM WHERE THEY'VE BEEN BILLETED...
WHERE?
HEH HEH HEH HEH, THE OLD COWSHED--!
...AND WHO ARE YOU?
UM, LIEUTENANT ANNA KHARKOVA, COMRADE GUARDS-MAJOR.
AND WHAT IS THAT, EXACTLY?
A CUSHION, COMRADE GUARDS-MAJOR.
I CAN SEE IT'S A CUSHION. WHAT ARE YOU DOING WITH IT HERE?
IT'S SO I CAN SEE OUT OF THE COCKPIT, COMRADE GUARDS-MAJOR. I'M NOT VERY BIG.
GIVE ME STRENGTH.
I THINK HE LIKES YOU.

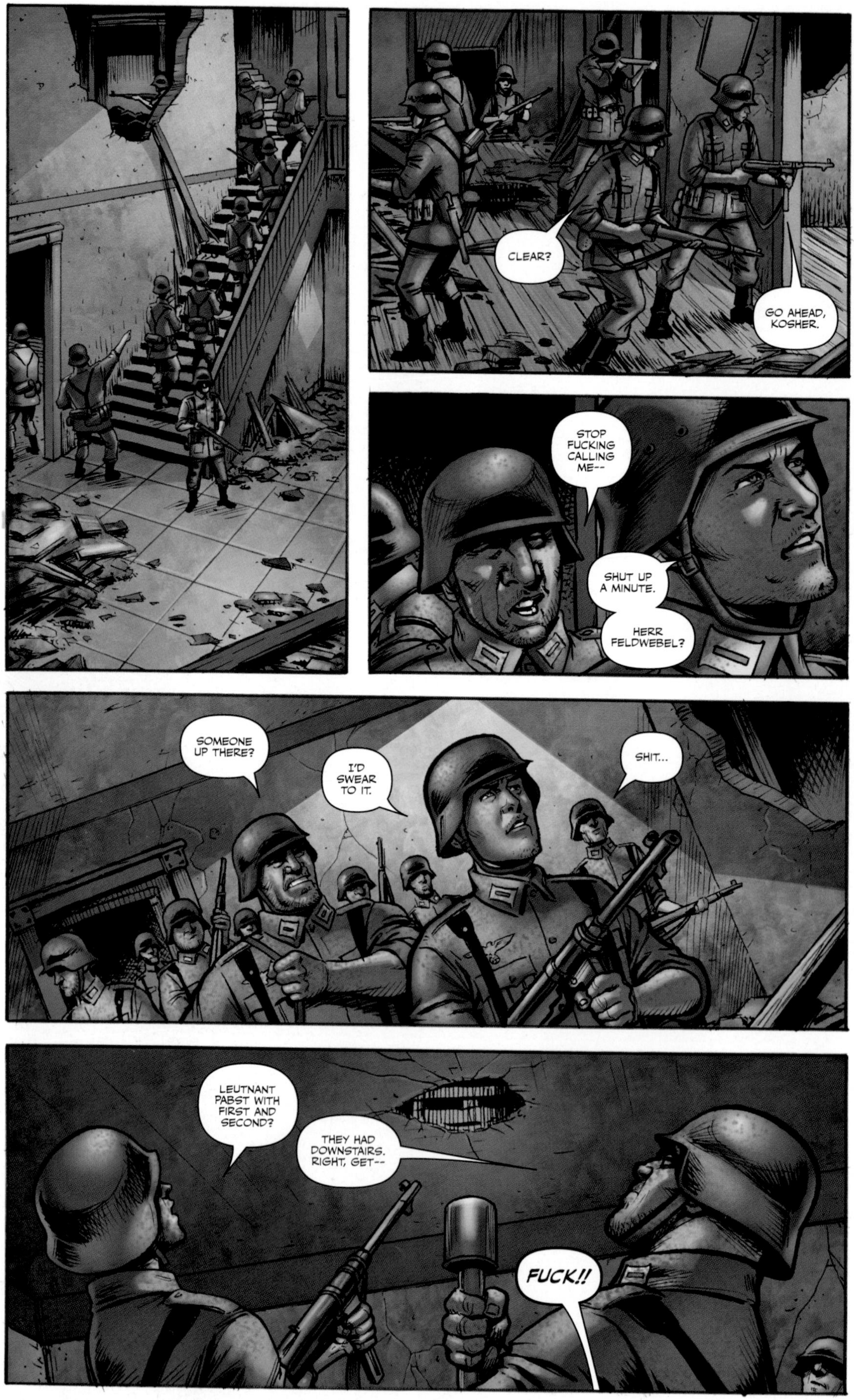
CLEAR?
GO AHEAD, KOSHER.
STOP FUCKING CALLING ME--
SHUT UP A MINUTE.
HERR FELDWEBEL?
SOMEONE UP THERE?
I'D SWEAR TO IT.
SHIT...
LEUTNANT PABST WITH FIRST AND SECOND?
THEY HAD DOWNSTAIRS. RIGHT, GET--
FUCK!!

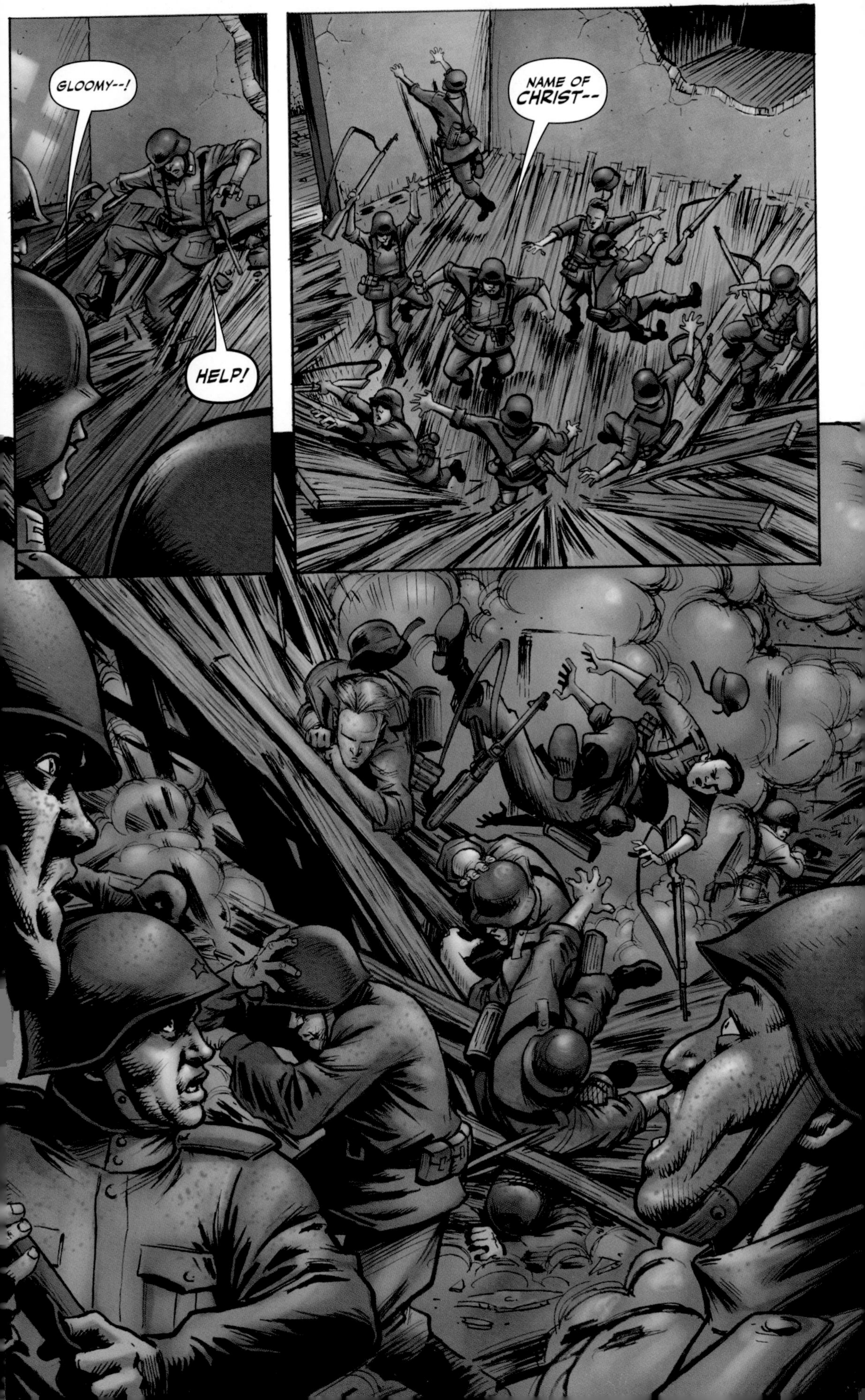
GLOOMY--!
HELP!
NAME OF CHRIST--

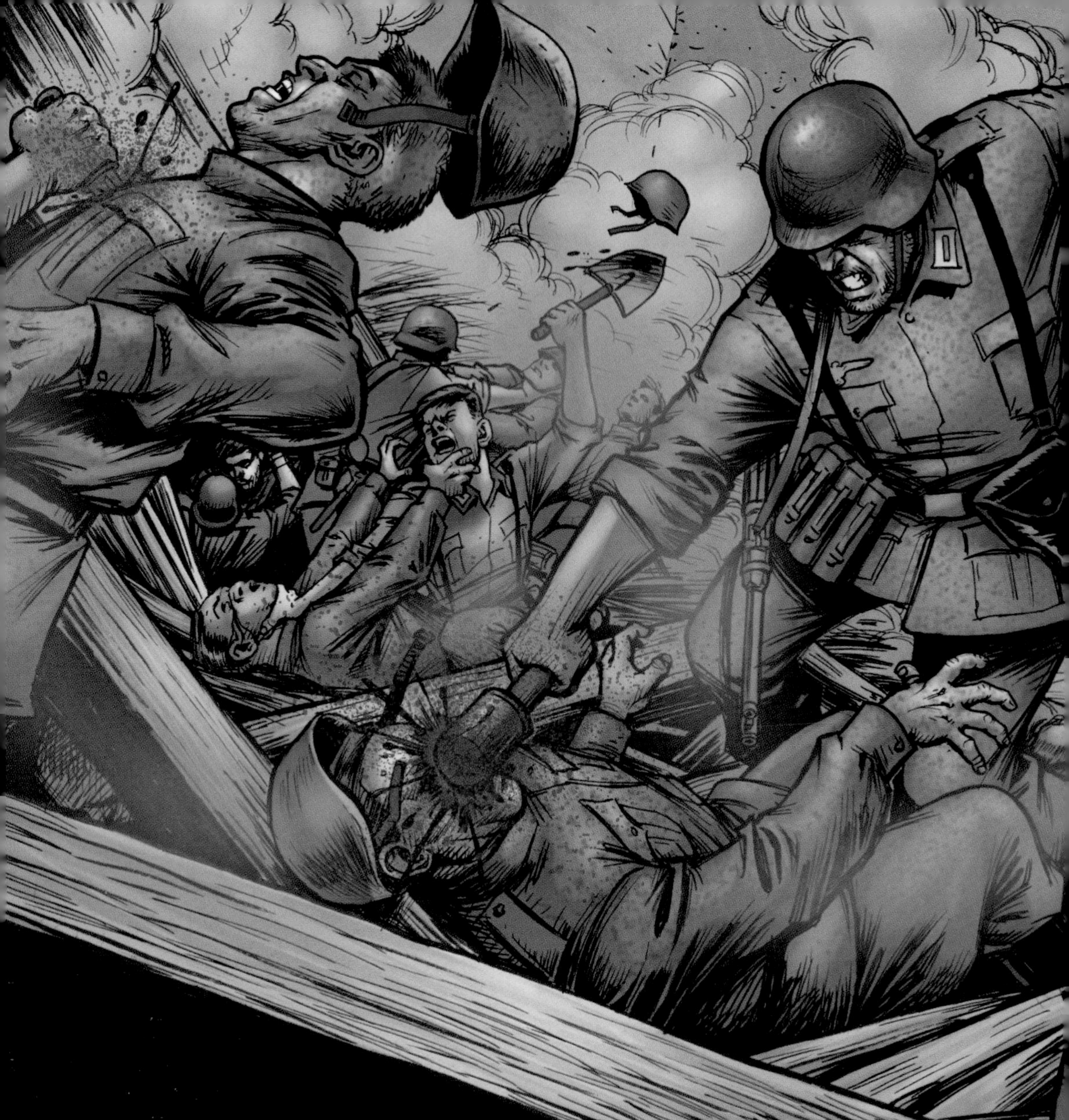

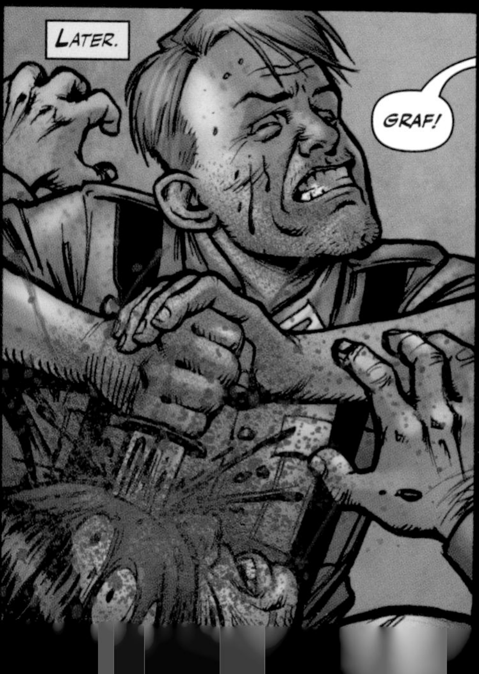
LATER.
GRAF!

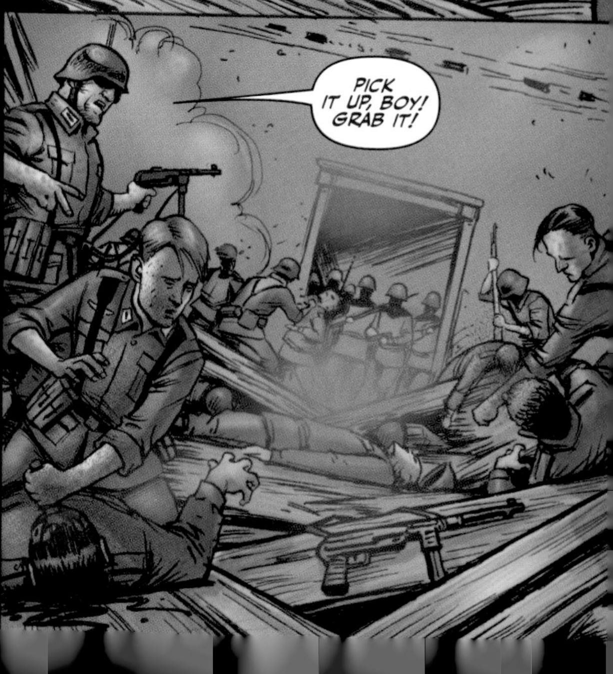
PICK IT UP, BOY! GRAB IT!

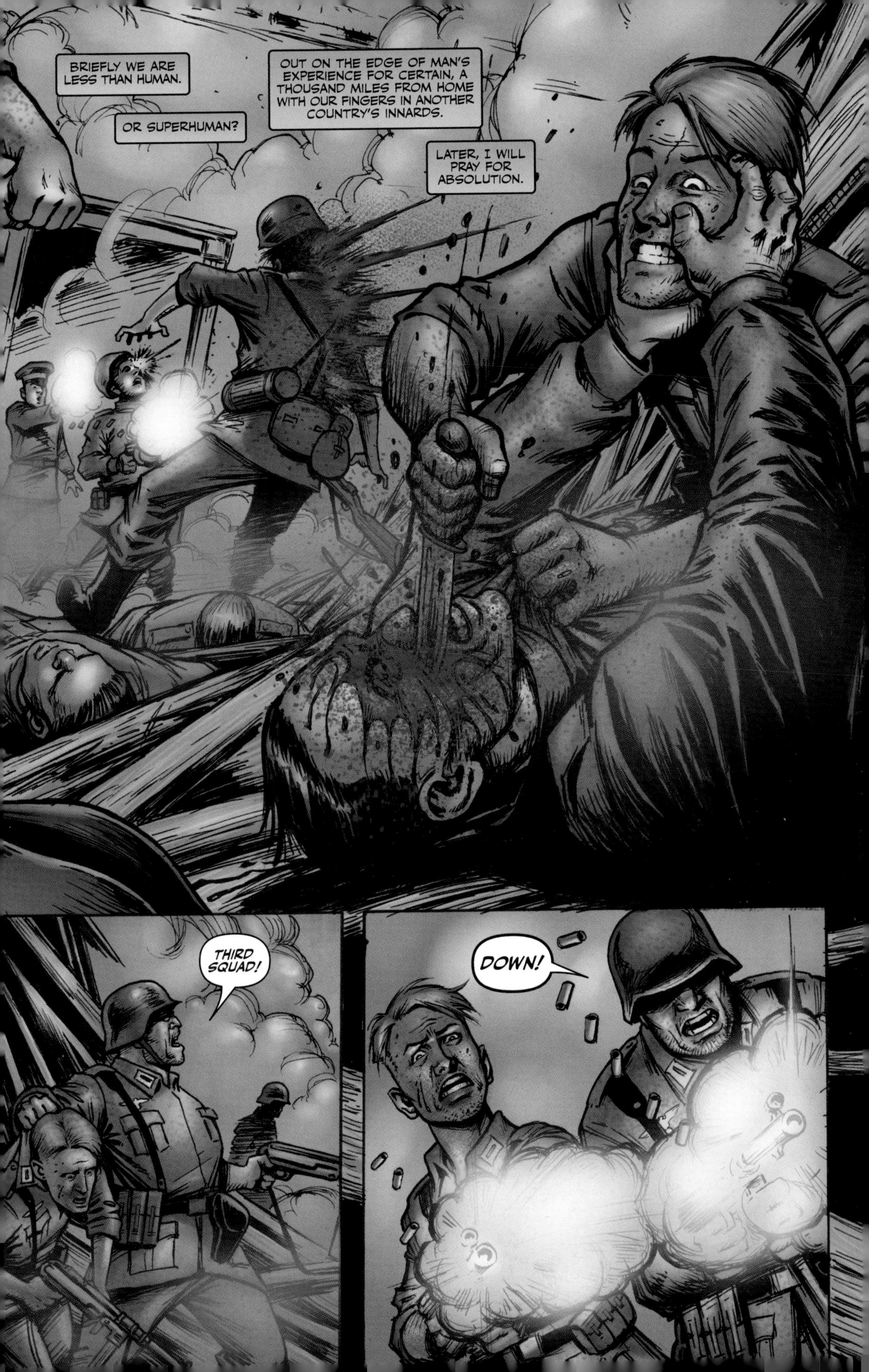
BRIEFLY WE ARE LESS THAN HUMAN.
OR SUPERHUMAN?
OUT ON THE EDGE OF MAN'S EXPERIENCE FOR CERTAIN, A THOUSAND MILES FROM HOME WITH OUR FINGERS IN ANOTHER COUNTRY'S INNARDS.
LATER, I WILL PRAY FOR ABSOLUTION.
THIRD SQUAD!
DOWN!

IT *STILL* REEKS OF MANURE.

LOOK WHAT THEY THINK OF US. WE'RE COWS TO THEM, WE'RE A SQUADRON OF FLYING COWS...

CAPTAIN OSIPOVA WANTS ME TO FETCH SOME COFFEE. COMING?

THE MEN WILL COME AROUND, ZOYA. IT'S HARD FOR THEM, THEY LOOK AT US AND SEE THEIR SISTERS OR THEIR SWEETHEARTS. PREMIER STALIN HIMSELF HAS SAID WE ARE THEIR EQUALS; IT'S A FOUNDING PRINCIPLE OF MARXIST-LENINISM...

OH, WE'RE THEIR EQUALS, ARE WE?

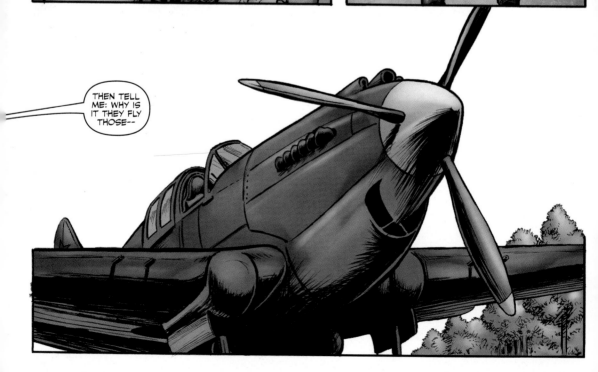

THEN TELL ME: WHY IS IT THEY FLY THOSE--

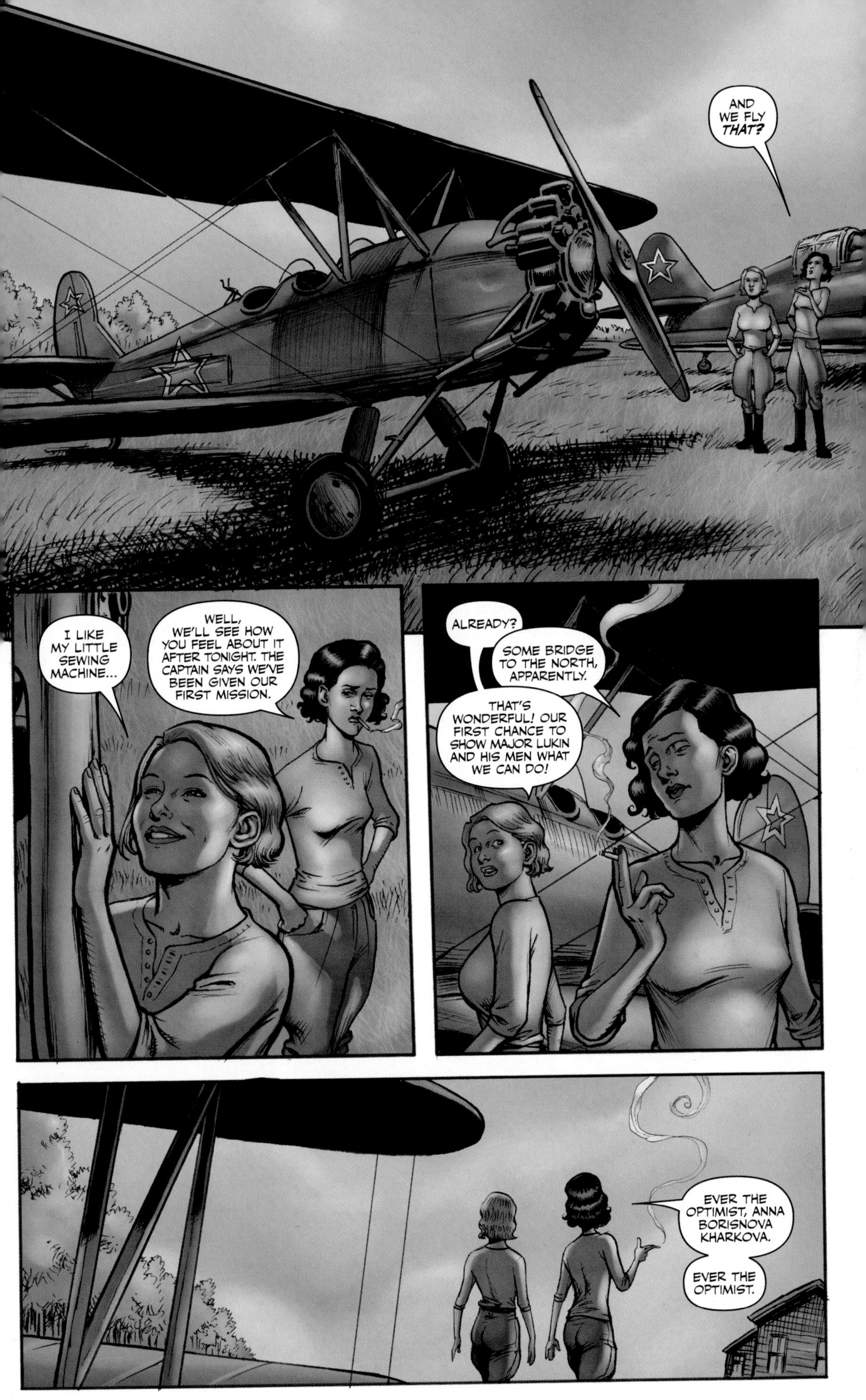
AND WE FLY *THAT?*
I LIKE MY LITTLE SEWING MACHINE...
WELL, WE'LL SEE HOW YOU FEEL ABOUT IT AFTER TONIGHT. THE CAPTAIN SAYS WE'VE BEEN GIVEN OUR FIRST MISSION.
ALREADY?
SOME BRIDGE TO THE NORTH, APPARENTLY.
THAT'S WONDERFUL! OUR FIRST CHANCE TO SHOW MAJOR LUKIN AND HIS MEN WHAT WE CAN DO!
EVER THE OPTIMIST, ANNA BORISNOVA KHARKOVA.
EVER THE OPTIMIST.

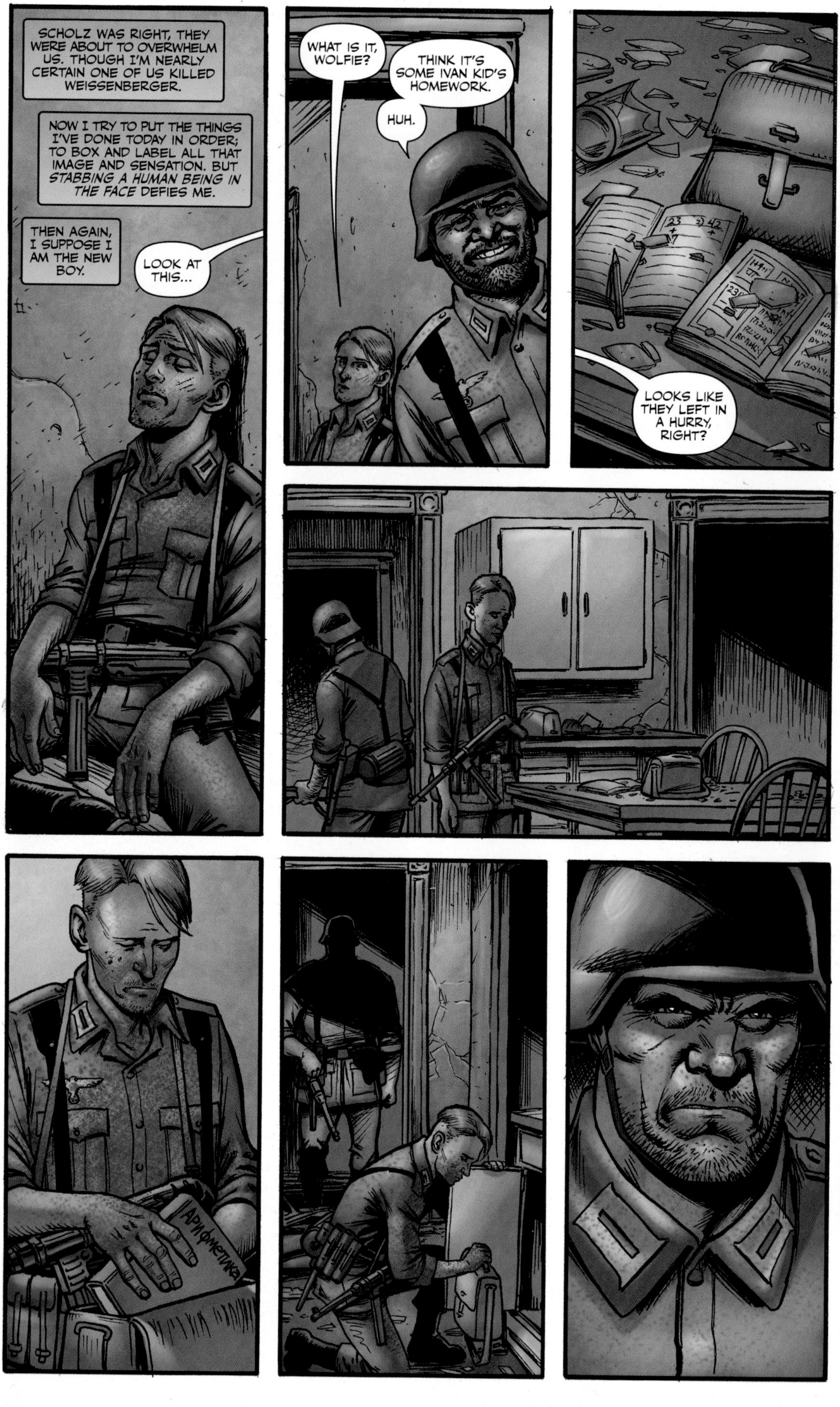
SCHOLZ WAS RIGHT, THEY WERE ABOUT TO OVERWHELM US. THOUGH I'M NEARLY CERTAIN ONE OF US KILLED WEISSENBERGER.
NOW I TRY TO PUT THE THINGS I'VE DONE TODAY IN ORDER; TO BOX AND LABEL ALL THAT IMAGE AND SENSATION. BUT *STABBING A HUMAN BEING IN THE FACE* DEFIES ME.
THEN AGAIN, I SUPPOSE I AM THE NEW BOY.
LOOK AT THIS...
WHAT IS IT, WOLFIE?
THINK IT'S SOME IVAN KID'S HOMEWORK.
HUH.
LOOKS LIKE THEY LEFT IN A HURRY, RIGHT?
АРИФМЕТИКА

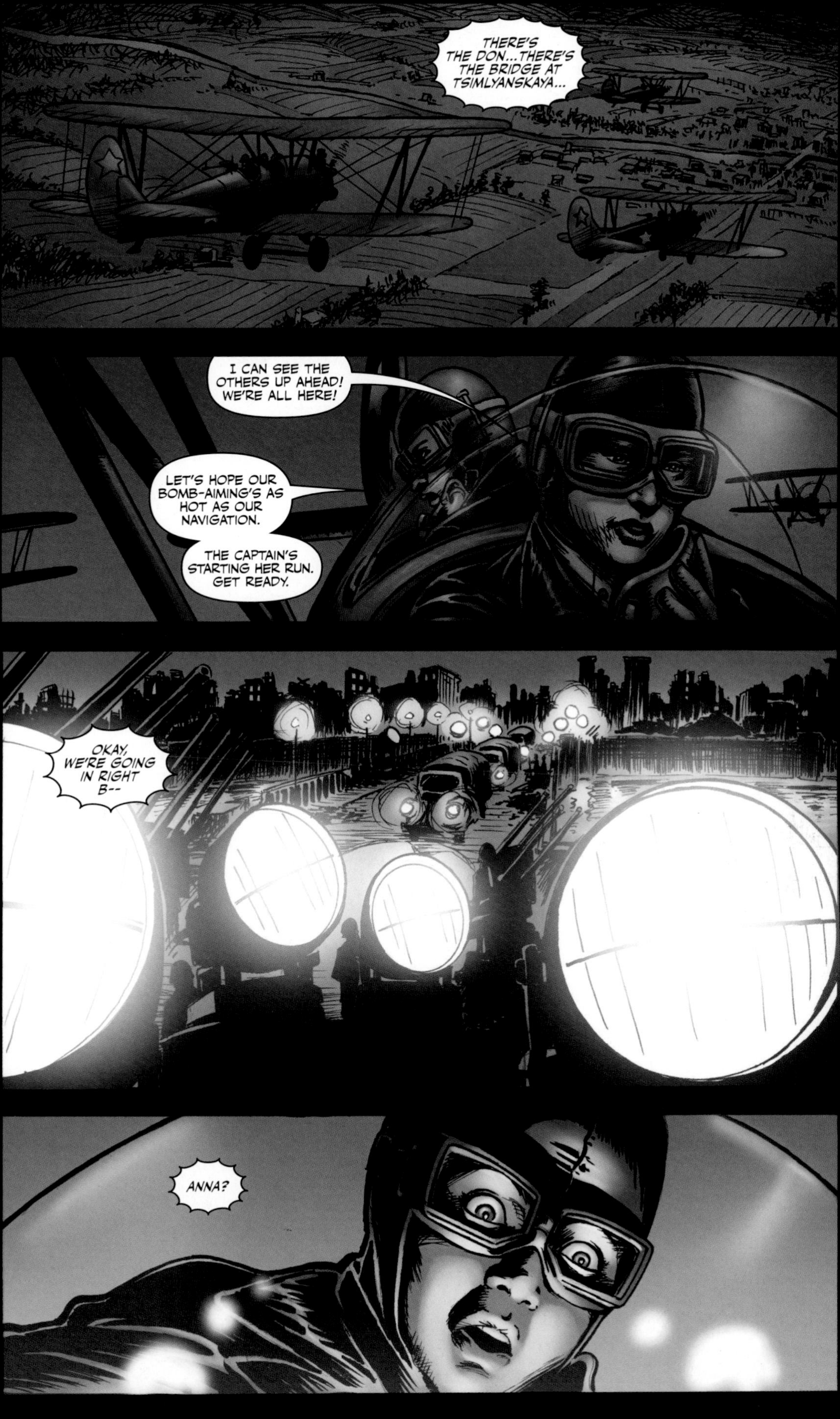
THERE'S THE DON...THERE'S THE BRIDGE AT TSIMLYANSKAYA...
I CAN SEE THE OTHERS UP AHEAD! WE'RE ALL HERE!
LET'S HOPE OUR BOMB-AIMING'S AS HOT AS OUR NAVIGATION.
THE CAPTAIN'S STARTING HER RUN. GET READY.
OKAY, WE'RE GOING IN RIGHT B--
ANNA?

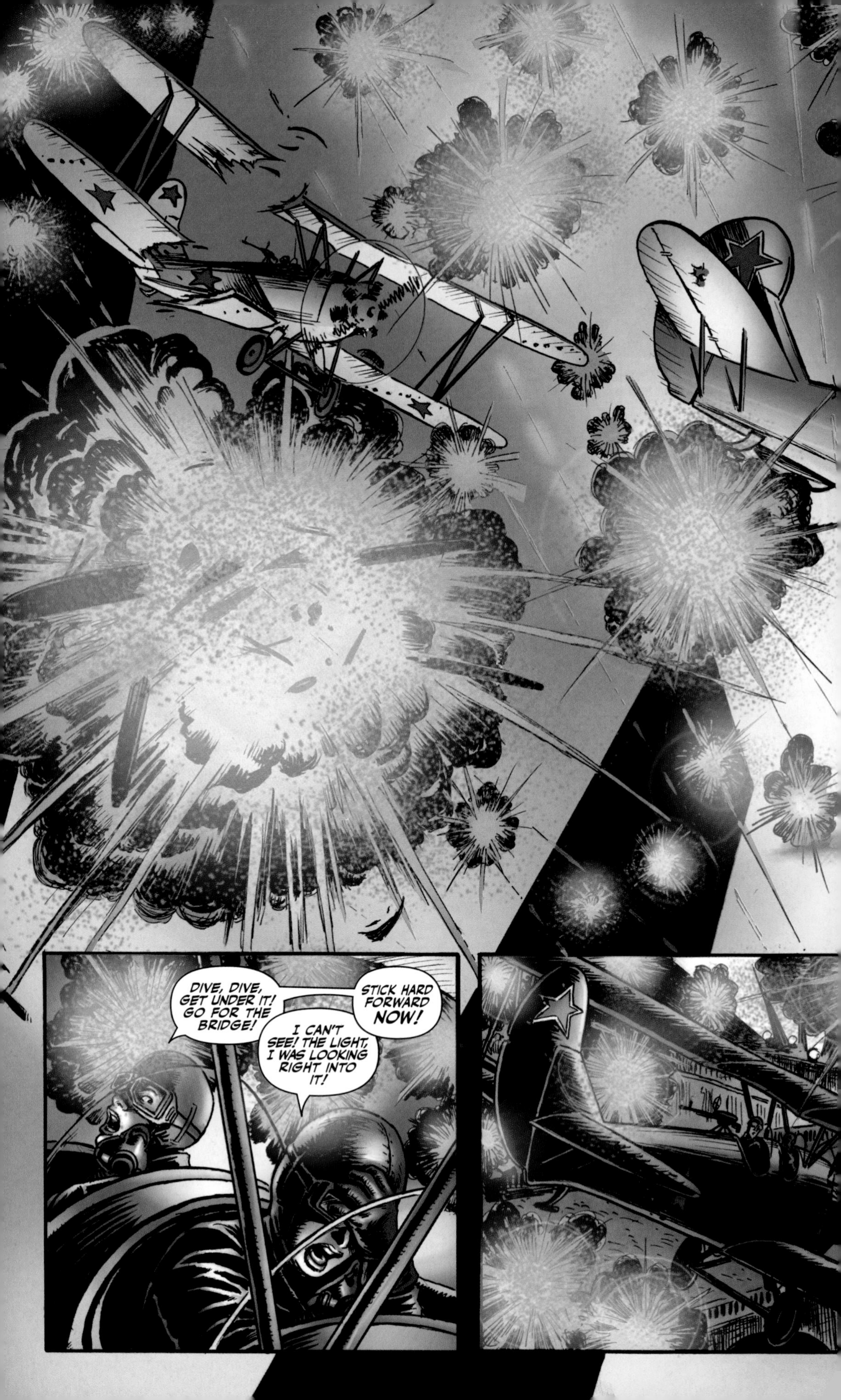
DIVE, DIVE, GET UNDER IT! GO FOR THE BRIDGE!
STICK HARD FORWARD NOW!
I CAN'T SEE! THE LIGHT, I WAS LOOKING RIGHT INTO IT!

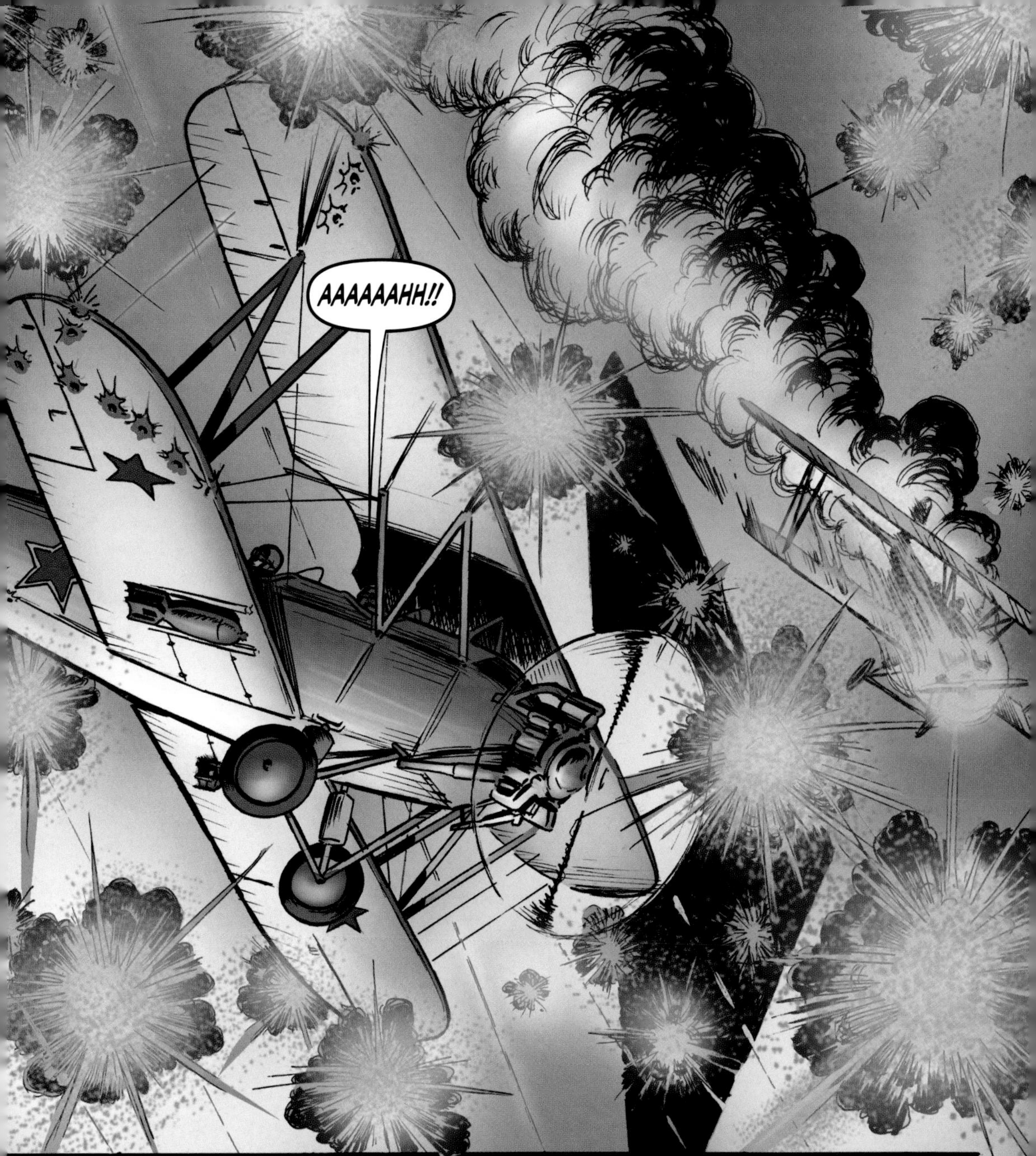
AAAAAAHH!!

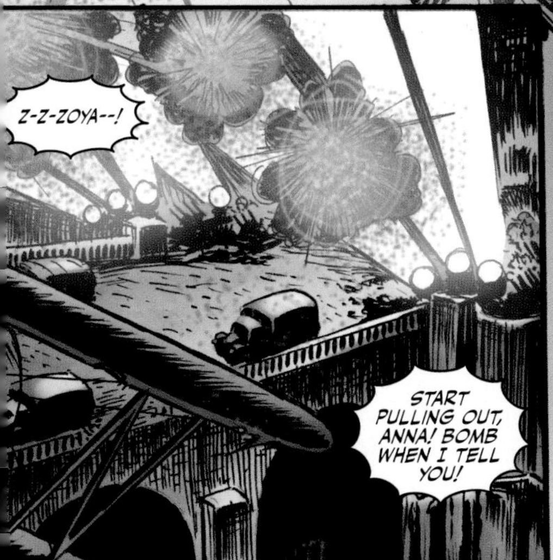
Z-Z-ZOYA--!
START PULLING OUT, ANNA! BOMB WHEN I TELL YOU!

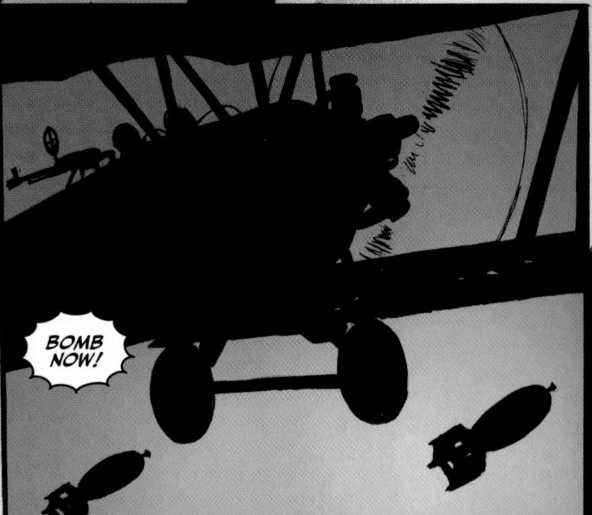
BOMB NOW!

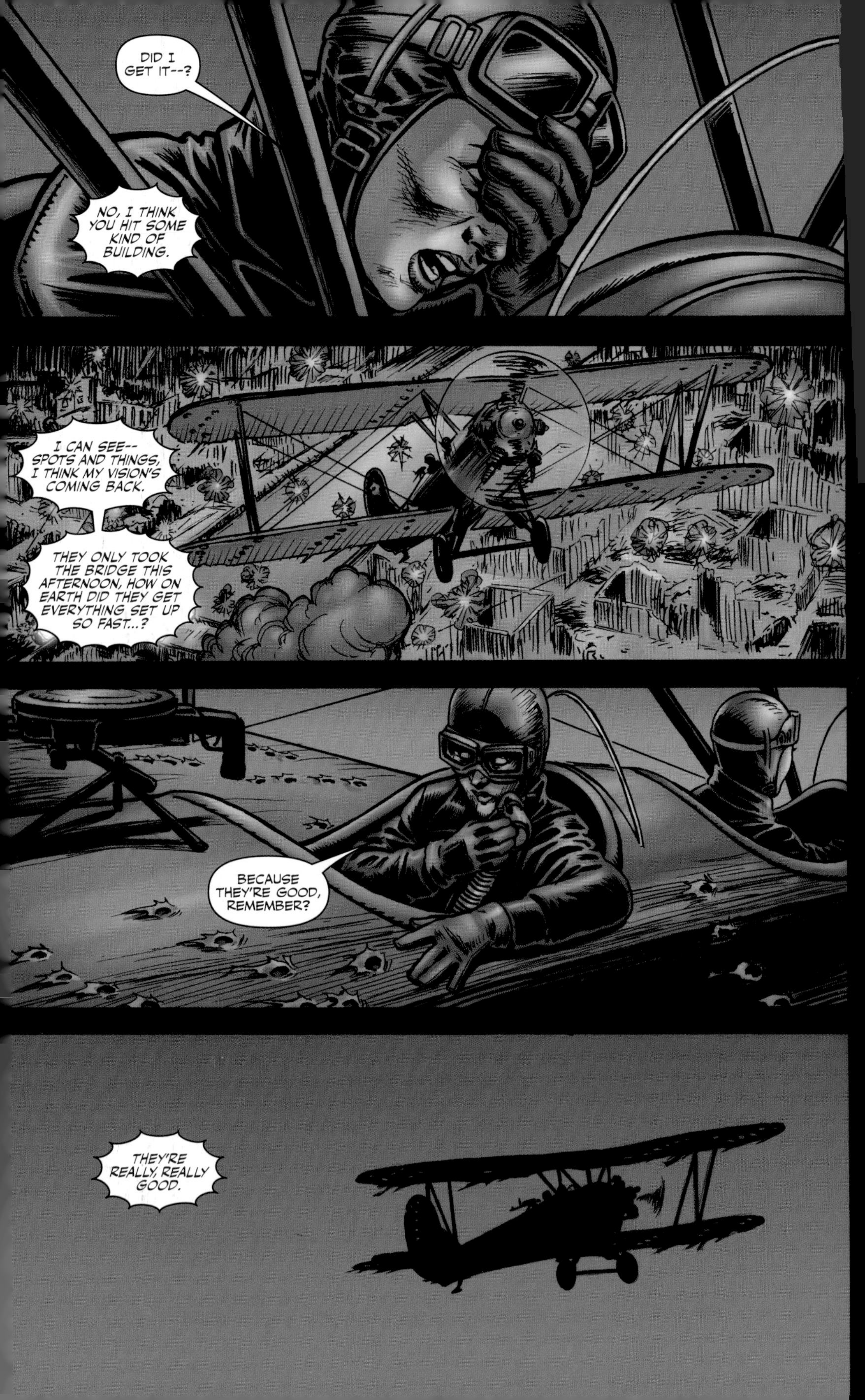
DID I GET IT--?
NO, I THINK YOU HIT SOME KIND OF BUILDING.
I CAN SEE-- SPOTS AND THINGS, I THINK MY VISION'S COMING BACK.
THEY ONLY TOOK THE BRIDGE THIS AFTERNOON, HOW ON EARTH DID THEY GET EVERYTHING SET UP SO FAST...?
BECAUSE THEY'RE GOOD, REMEMBER?
THEY'RE REALLY, REALLY GOOD.

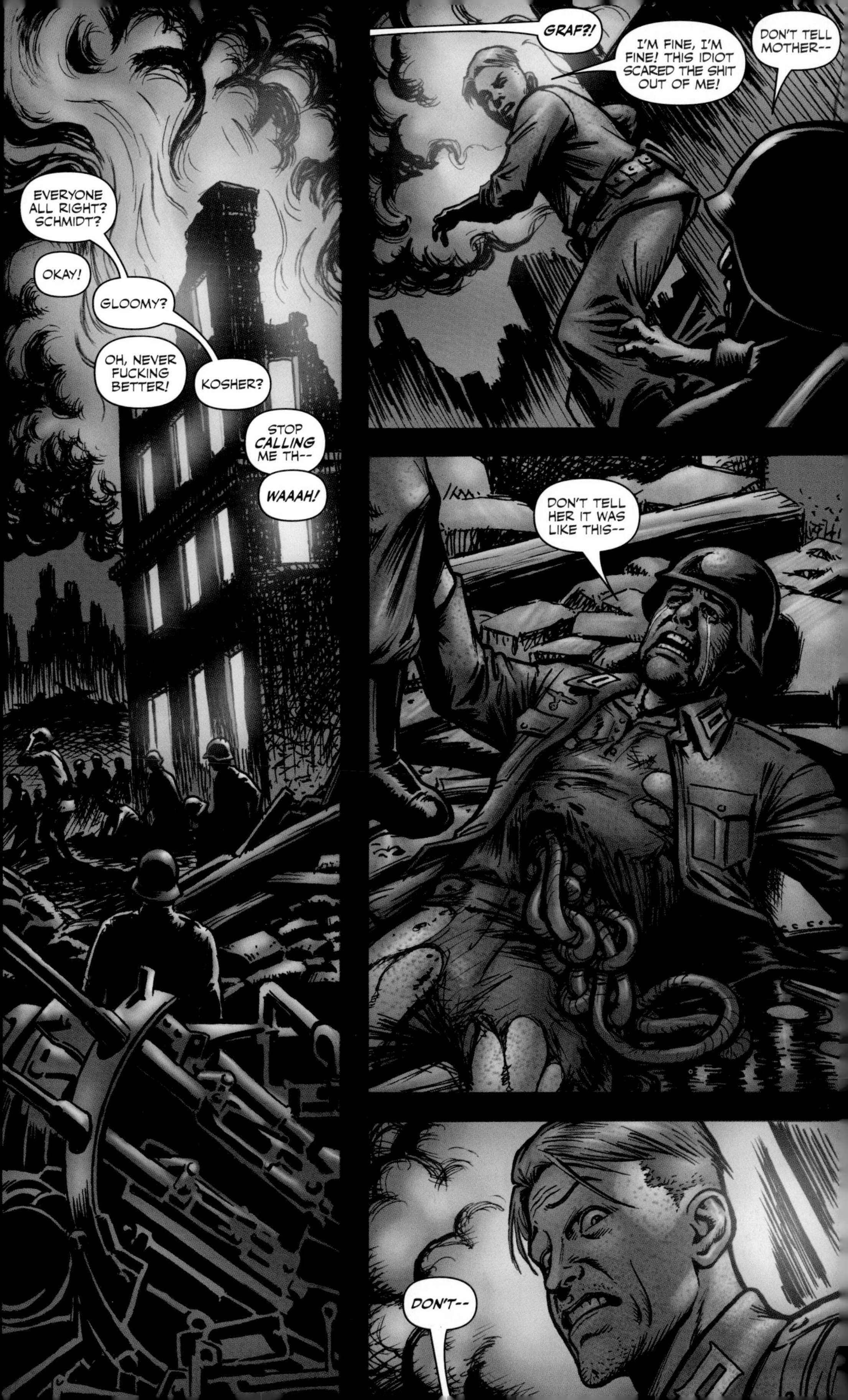
EVERYONE ALL RIGHT? SCHMIDT?
OKAY!
GLOOMY?
OH, NEVER FUCKING BETTER!
KOSHER?
STOP *CALLING* ME TH--
WAAAH!
GRAF?!
I'M FINE, I'M FINE! THIS IDIOT SCARED THE SHIT OUT OF ME!
DON'T TELL MOTHER--
DON'T TELL HER IT WAS LIKE THIS--
DON'T--

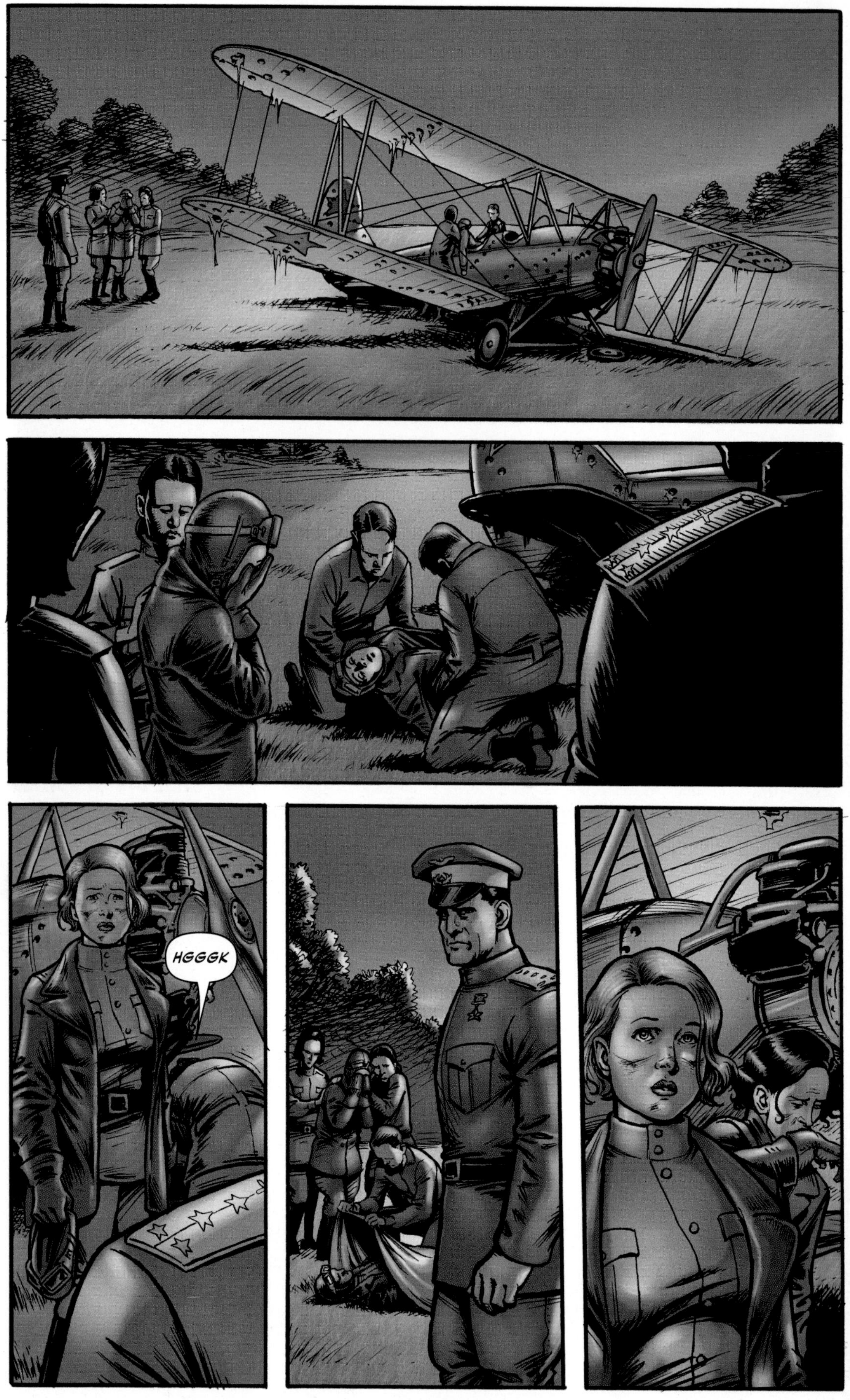
HGGGK

OKAY...? FINE. IT ISN'T THE BLOOD.

...WELL, IT IS.

IT'S THE BLOOD, AND VALENTINA LYING DEAD OVER THERE, AND THE *TERROR* OF FLYING INTO THAT FLAK. AND THE OTHER FOUR CREWS NOT COMING BACK AT ALL.

BUT REALLY IT'S THE STUPIDITY, ANNA. THAT'S WHAT'S GOT ME SO SICKENED.

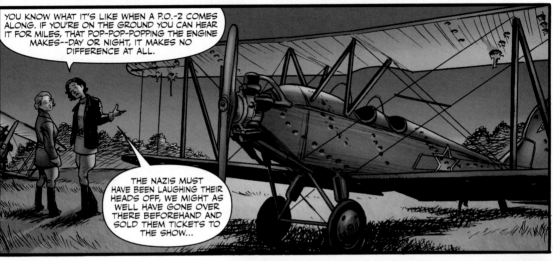

YOU KNOW WHAT IT'S LIKE WHEN A P.O.-2 COMES ALONG. IF YOU'RE ON THE GROUND YOU CAN HEAR IT FOR MILES, THAT POP-POP-POPPING THE ENGINE MAKES--DAY OR NIGHT, IT MAKES NO DIFFERENCE AT ALL.

THE NAZIS MUST HAVE BEEN LAUGHING THEIR HEADS OFF, WE MIGHT AS WELL HAVE GONE OVER THERE BEFOREHAND AND SOLD THEM TICKETS TO THE SHOW...

IT'S WAR, I SUPPOSE.

IT'S SUICIDE.

TWO MORE MISSIONS LIKE THAT AND WE'LL ALL BE DONE WITH, UNLESS WE CAN MAGICALLY STOP THEM FROM HEARING US COMING.

...OH NO.

NO, ZOYA.

PLEASE TELL ME YOU'RE JOKING.

IS THAT WHAT I THINK IT IS?

IS WHAT IS, KOSHER?

FOR THE LAST FUCKING TIME--

ARE YOU SCARED THE GESTAPO WILL OVERHEAR AND PICK YOU UP ON GENERAL PRINCIPLE?

WHERE...?

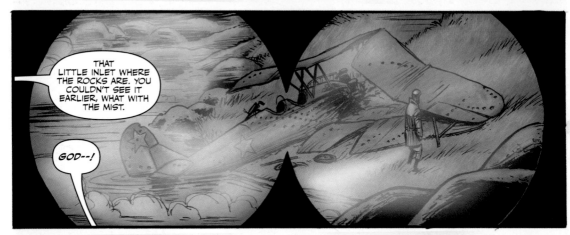

THAT LITTLE INLET WHERE THE ROCKS ARE. YOU COULDN'T SEE IT EARLIER, WHAT WITH THE MIST.

GOD--!

IT'S ONE OF THOSE FUCKERS FROM LAST NIGHT!

WEAPONS! NOW! I WANT THE IVAN SHITS ALIVE!

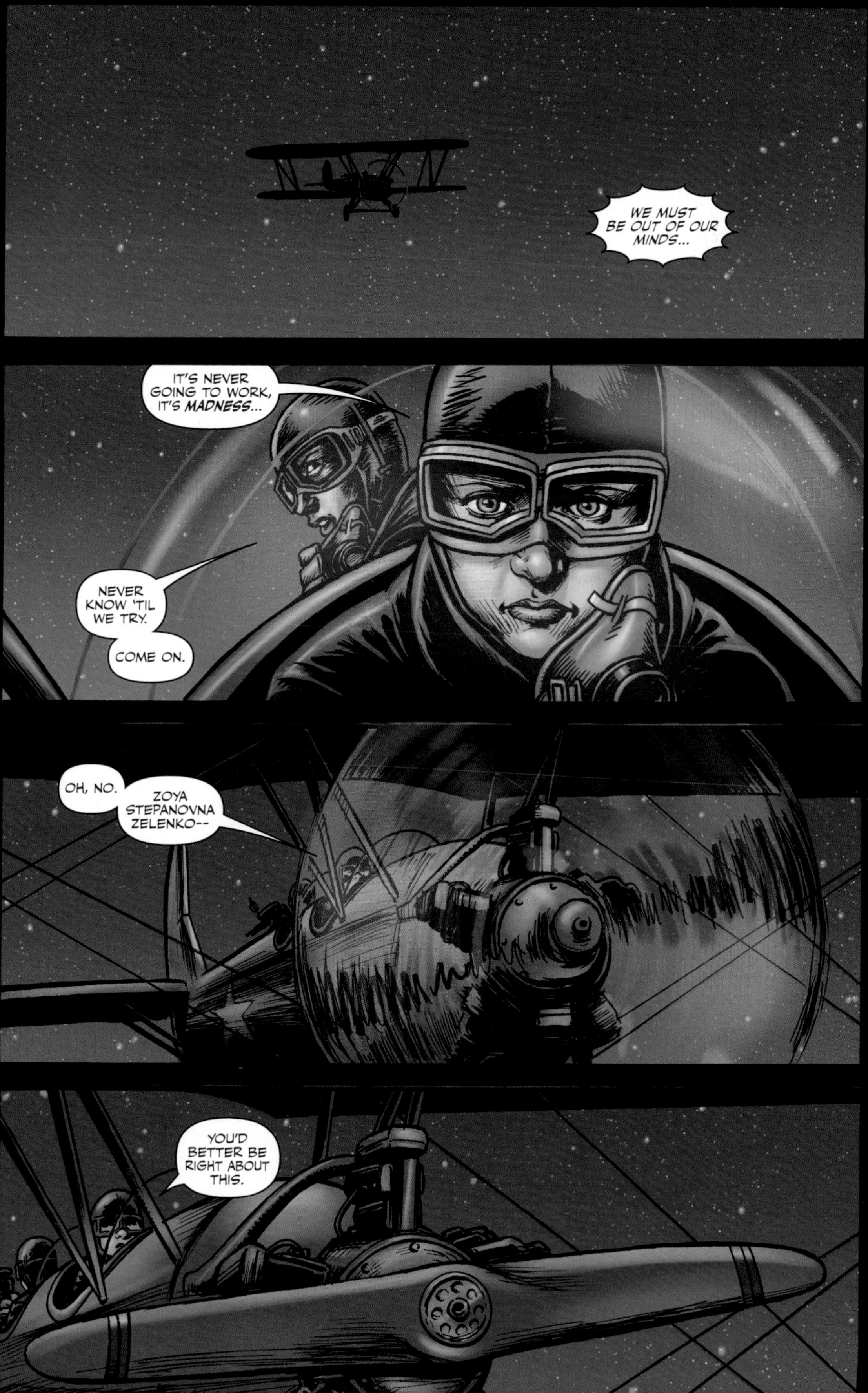
WE MUST BE OUT OF OUR MINDS...
IT'S NEVER GOING TO WORK, IT'S *MADNESS*...
NEVER KNOW 'TIL WE TRY.
COME ON.
OH, NO.
ZOYA STEPANOVNA ZELENKO--
YOU'D BETTER BE RIGHT ABOUT THIS.

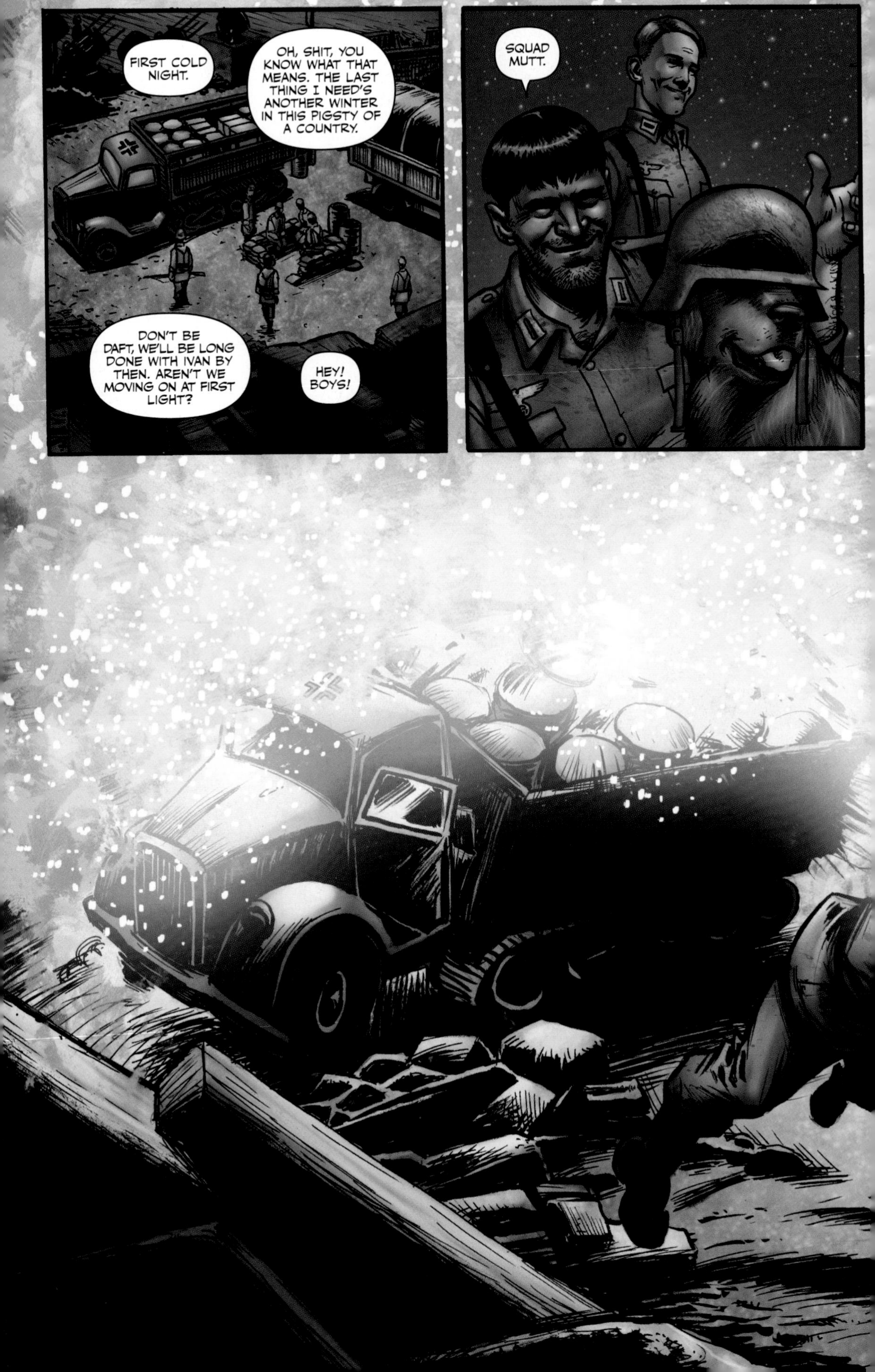
FIRST COLD NIGHT.
OH, SHIT, YOU KNOW WHAT THAT MEANS. THE LAST THING I NEED'S ANOTHER WINTER IN THIS PIGSTY OF A COUNTRY.
DON'T BE DAFT, WE'LL BE LONG DONE WITH IVAN BY THEN. AREN'T WE MOVING ON AT FIRST LIGHT?
HEY! BOYS!
SQUAD MUTT.

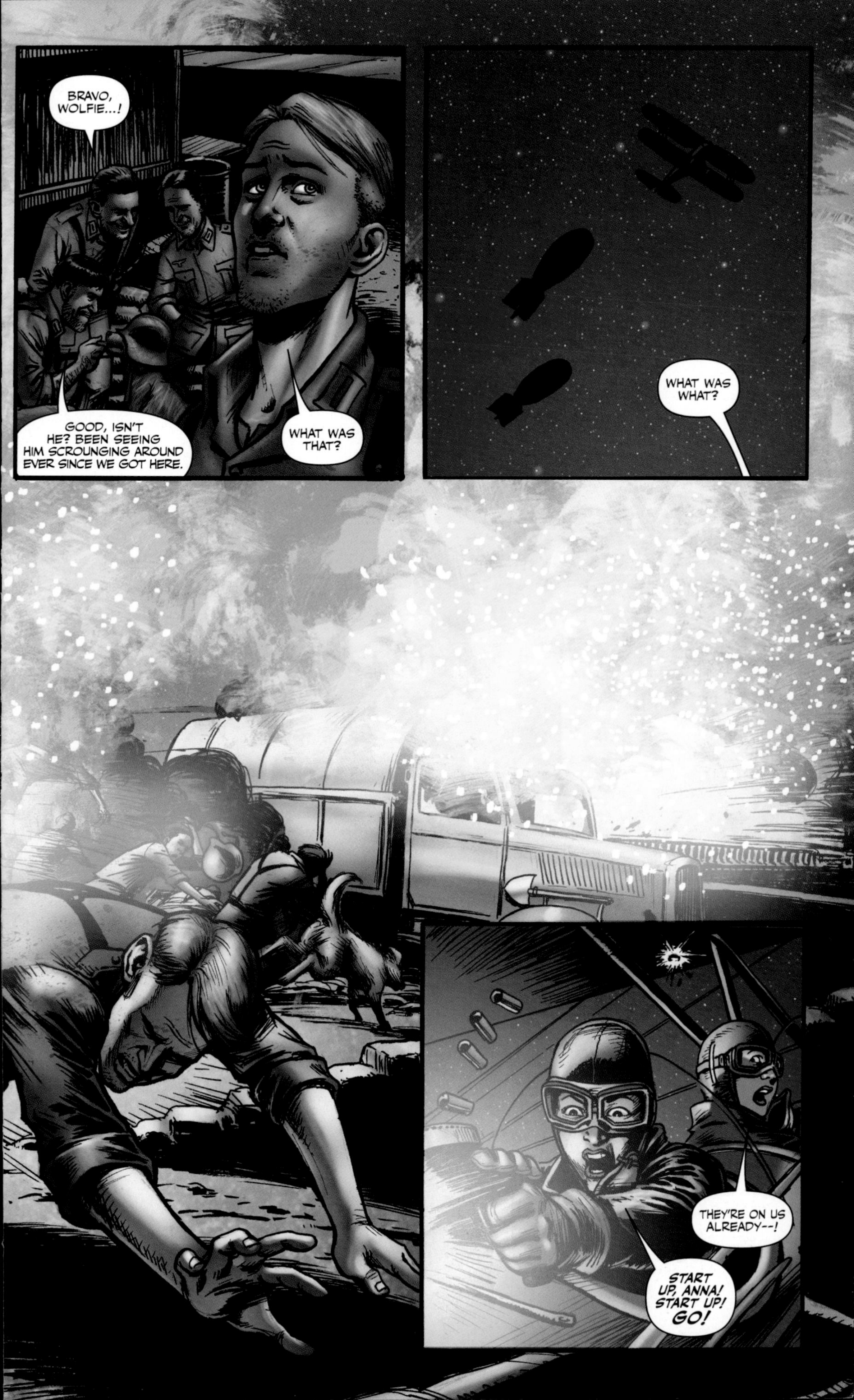
BRAVO, WOLFIE...!
GOOD, ISN'T HE? BEEN SEEING HIM SCROUNGING AROUND EVER SINCE WE GOT HERE.
WHAT WAS THAT?
WHAT WAS WHAT?
THEY'RE ON US ALREADY--!
START UP, ANNA! START UP! GO!

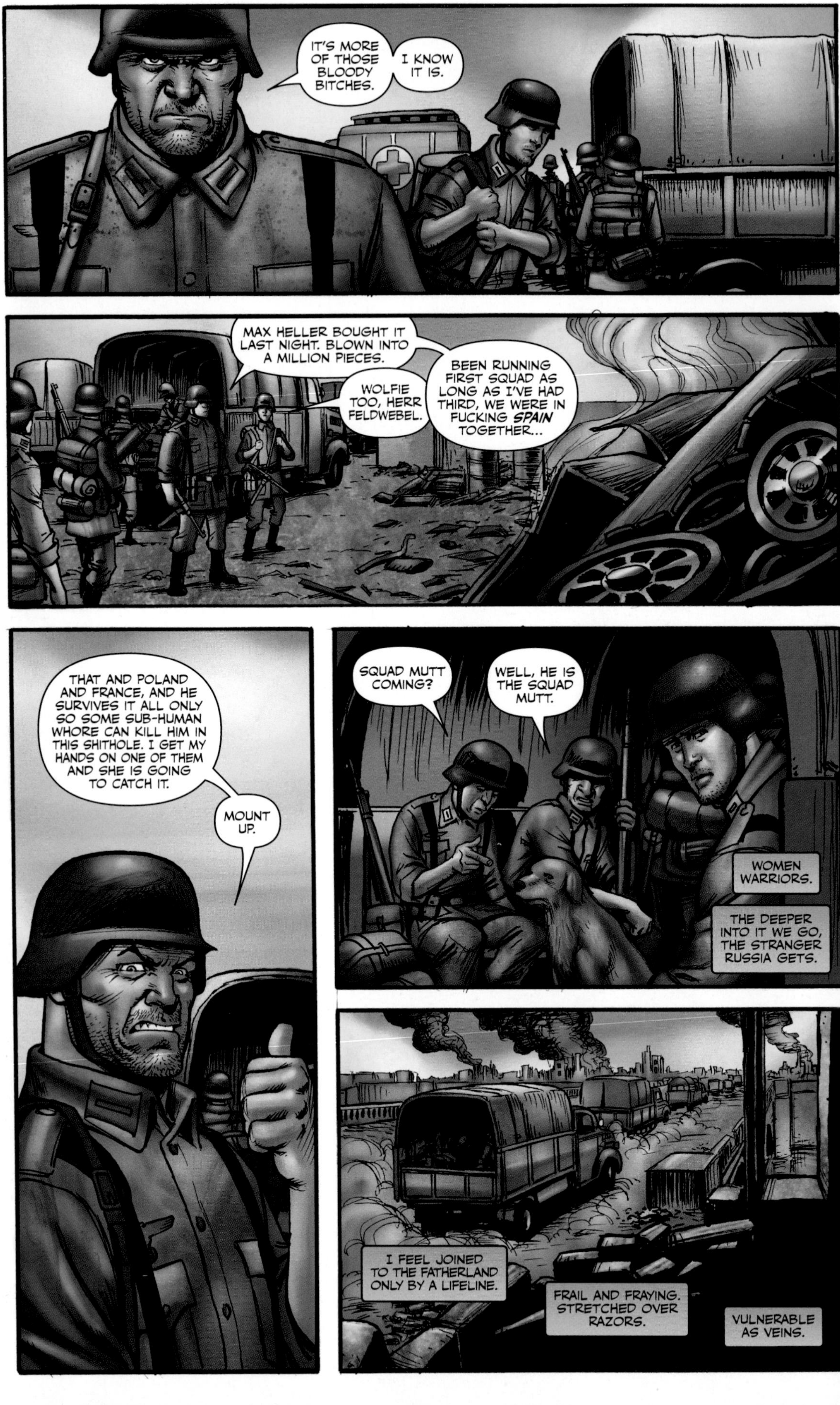
IT'S MORE OF THOSE BLOODY BITCHES.
I KNOW IT IS.
MAX HELLER BOUGHT IT LAST NIGHT. BLOWN INTO A MILLION PIECES.
WOLFIE TOO, HERR FELDWEBEL.
BEEN RUNNING FIRST SQUAD AS LONG AS I'VE HAD THIRD, WE WERE IN FUCKING SPAIN TOGETHER...
THAT AND POLAND AND FRANCE, AND HE SURVIVES IT ALL ONLY SO SOME SUB-HUMAN WHORE CAN KILL HIM IN THIS SHITHOLE. I GET MY HANDS ON ONE OF THEM AND SHE IS GOING TO CATCH IT.
MOUNT UP.
SQUAD MUTT COMING?
WELL, HE IS THE SQUAD MUTT.
WOMEN WARRIORS.
THE DEEPER INTO IT WE GO, THE STRANGER RUSSIA GETS.
I FEEL JOINED TO THE FATHERLAND ONLY BY A LIFELINE.
FRAIL AND FRAYING. STRETCHED OVER RAZORS.
VULNERABLE AS VEINS.

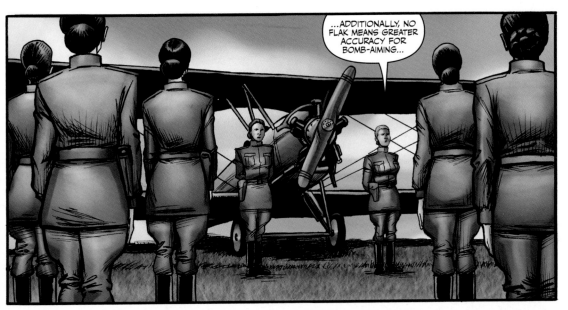

...ADDITIONALLY, NO FLAK MEANS GREATER ACCURACY FOR BOMB-AIMING...

SO YOU CAN AFFORD TO TAKE YOUR TIME AND CHECK YOUR TARGET. AFTER ALL, WE WON'T ALWAYS HAVE THE RIVER FOR A LANDMARK.

START THE ENGINE THE INSTANT THE BOMBS ARE GONE. PUT YOUR NOSE DOWN AND GET OUT AS FAST AS YOU CAN, THEY PICKED US UP STRAIGHTAWAY LAST NIGHT.

COMRADE CAPTAIN?

THANK YOU, COMRADE LIEUTENANT.

REMEMBER ALSO THAT A GLIDING ATTACK HAS ITS OWN LIMITATIONS. ONLY THE FIRST AIRCRAFT WILL ACHIEVE ANY MEASURE OF SURPRISE, AFTER THAT THE NAZIS WILL BE WIDE AWAKE.

NOW, I'M NOT GOING TO LAY DOWN ANY HARD AND FAST RULES; IT'S UP TO EACH CREW WHETHER OR NOT THEY ADOPT LIEUTENANT KHARKOVA'S TACTICS--

EXCUSE ME, COMRADE CAPTAIN?

BUT IT'S CERTAINLY AN IDEA WORTH--

COMRADE CAPTAIN?

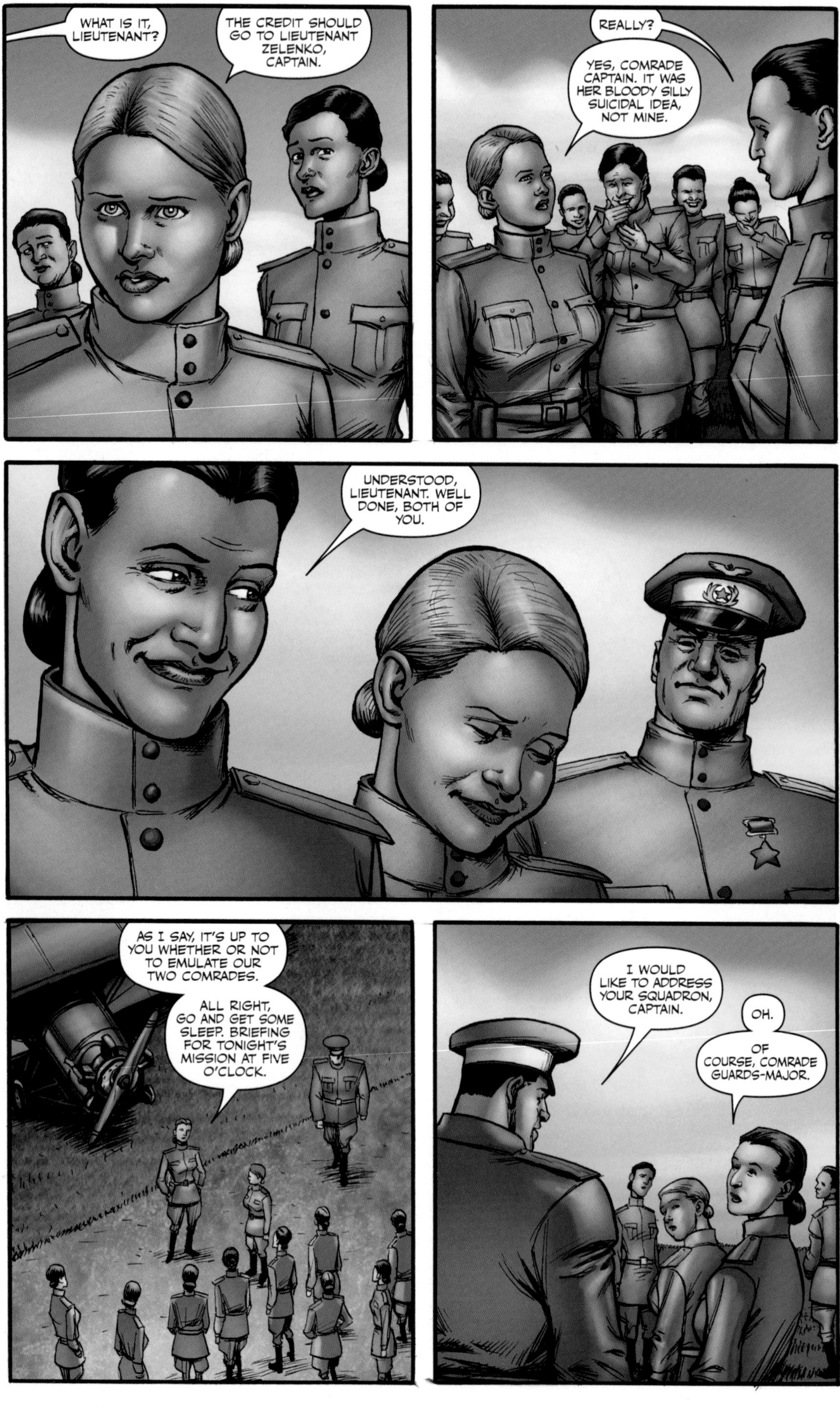
WHAT IS IT, LIEUTENANT?
THE CREDIT SHOULD GO TO LIEUTENANT ZELENKO, CAPTAIN.
REALLY?
YES, COMRADE CAPTAIN. IT WAS HER BLOODY SILLY SUICIDAL IDEA, NOT MINE.
UNDERSTOOD, LIEUTENANT. WELL DONE, BOTH OF YOU.
AS I SAY, IT'S UP TO YOU WHETHER OR NOT TO EMULATE OUR TWO COMRADES.
ALL RIGHT, GO AND GET SOME SLEEP. BRIEFING FOR TONIGHT'S MISSION AT FIVE O'CLOCK.
I WOULD LIKE TO ADDRESS YOUR SQUADRON, CAPTAIN.
OH.
OF COURSE, COMRADE GUARDS-MAJOR.

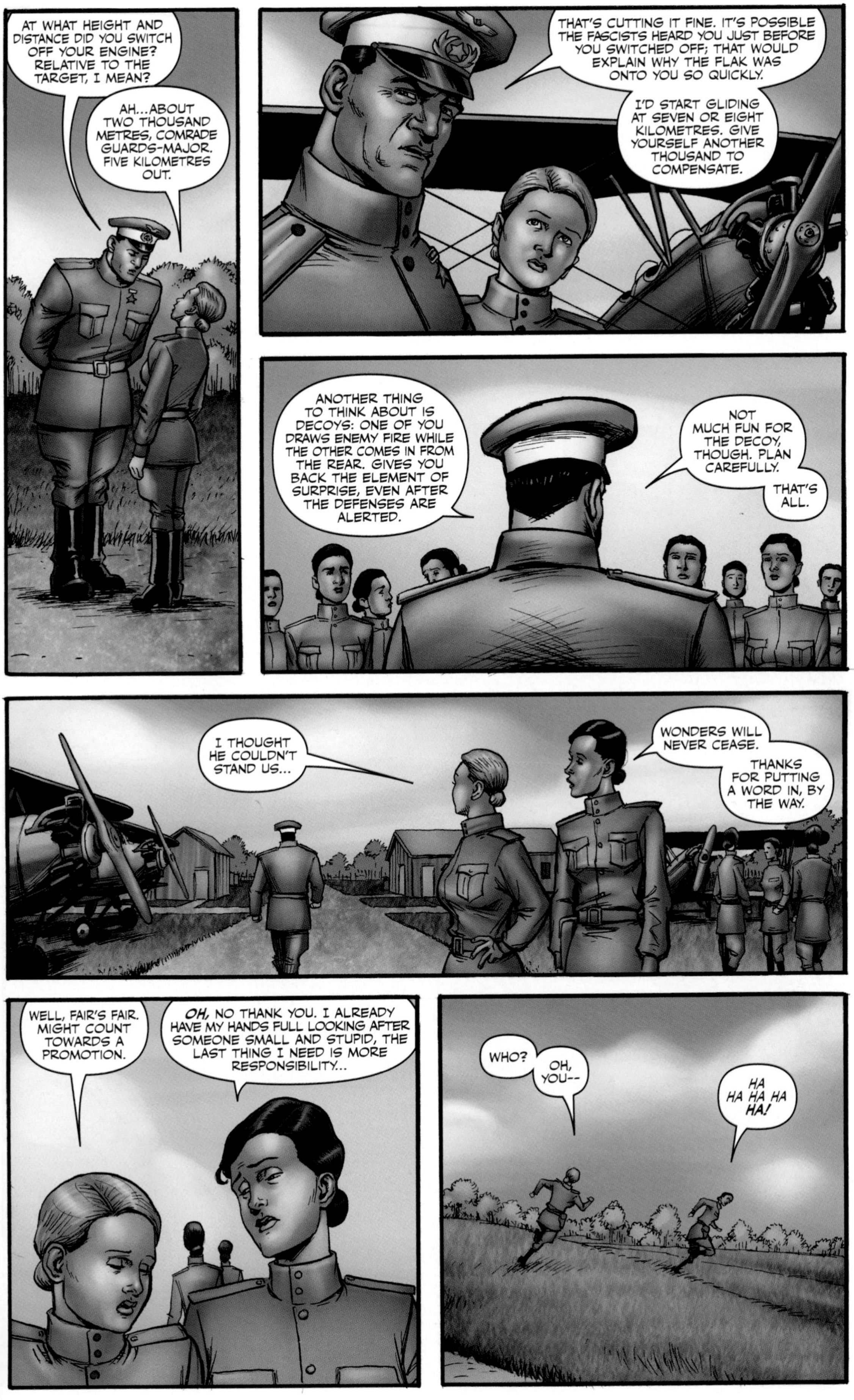
AT WHAT HEIGHT AND DISTANCE DID YOU SWITCH OFF YOUR ENGINE? RELATIVE TO THE TARGET, I MEAN?
AH...ABOUT TWO THOUSAND METRES, COMRADE GUARDS-MAJOR. FIVE KILOMETRES OUT.
THAT'S CUTTING IT FINE. IT'S POSSIBLE THE FASCISTS HEARD YOU JUST BEFORE YOU SWITCHED OFF; THAT WOULD EXPLAIN WHY THE FLAK WAS ONTO YOU SO QUICKLY.
I'D START GLIDING AT SEVEN OR EIGHT KILOMETRES. GIVE YOURSELF ANOTHER THOUSAND TO COMPENSATE.
ANOTHER THING TO THINK ABOUT IS DECOYS: ONE OF YOU DRAWS ENEMY FIRE WHILE THE OTHER COMES IN FROM THE REAR. GIVES YOU BACK THE ELEMENT OF SURPRISE, EVEN AFTER THE DEFENSES ARE ALERTED.
NOT MUCH FUN FOR THE DECOY, THOUGH. PLAN CAREFULLY.
THAT'S ALL.
I THOUGHT HE COULDN'T STAND US...
WONDERS WILL NEVER CEASE.
THANKS FOR PUTTING A WORD IN, BY THE WAY.
WELL, FAIR'S FAIR. MIGHT COUNT TOWARDS A PROMOTION.
OH, NO THANK YOU. I ALREADY HAVE MY HANDS FULL LOOKING AFTER SOMEONE SMALL AND STUPID, THE LAST THING I NEED IS MORE RESPONSIBILITY...
WHO?
OH, YOU--
HA HA HA HA HA!

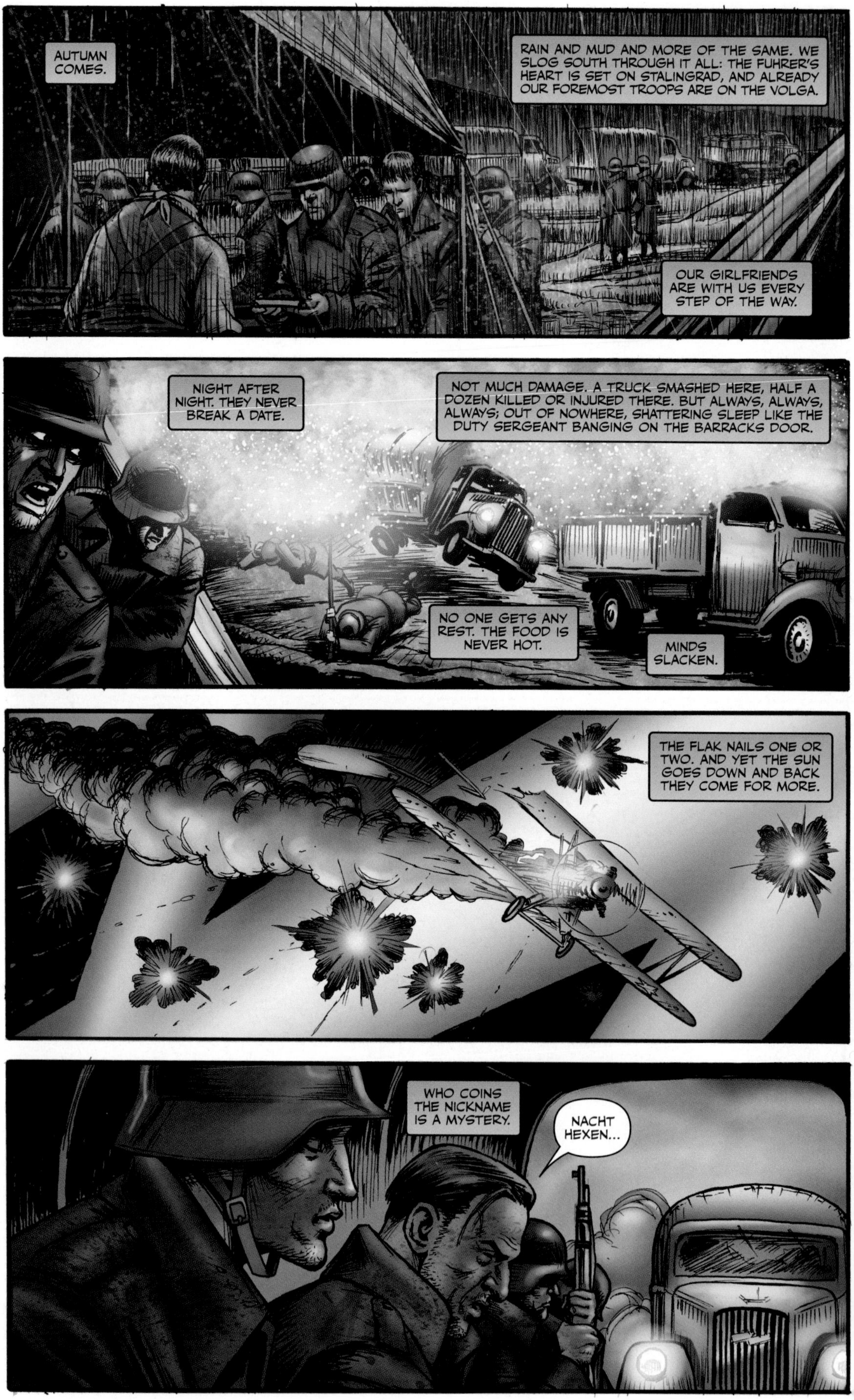
AUTUMN COMES.
RAIN AND MUD AND MORE OF THE SAME. WE SLOG SOUTH THROUGH IT ALL: THE FUHRER'S HEART IS SET ON STALINGRAD, AND ALREADY OUR FOREMOST TROOPS ARE ON THE VOLGA.
OUR GIRLFRIENDS ARE WITH US EVERY STEP OF THE WAY.
NIGHT AFTER NIGHT. THEY NEVER BREAK A DATE.
NOT MUCH DAMAGE. A TRUCK SMASHED HERE, HALF A DOZEN KILLED OR INJURED THERE. BUT ALWAYS, ALWAYS, ALWAYS; OUT OF NOWHERE, SHATTERING SLEEP LIKE THE DUTY SERGEANT BANGING ON THE BARRACKS DOOR.
NO ONE GETS ANY REST. THE FOOD IS NEVER HOT.
MINDS SLACKEN.
THE FLAK NAILS ONE OR TWO. AND YET THE SUN GOES DOWN AND BACK THEY COME FOR MORE.
WHO COINS THE NICKNAME IS A MYSTERY.
NACHT HEXEN...

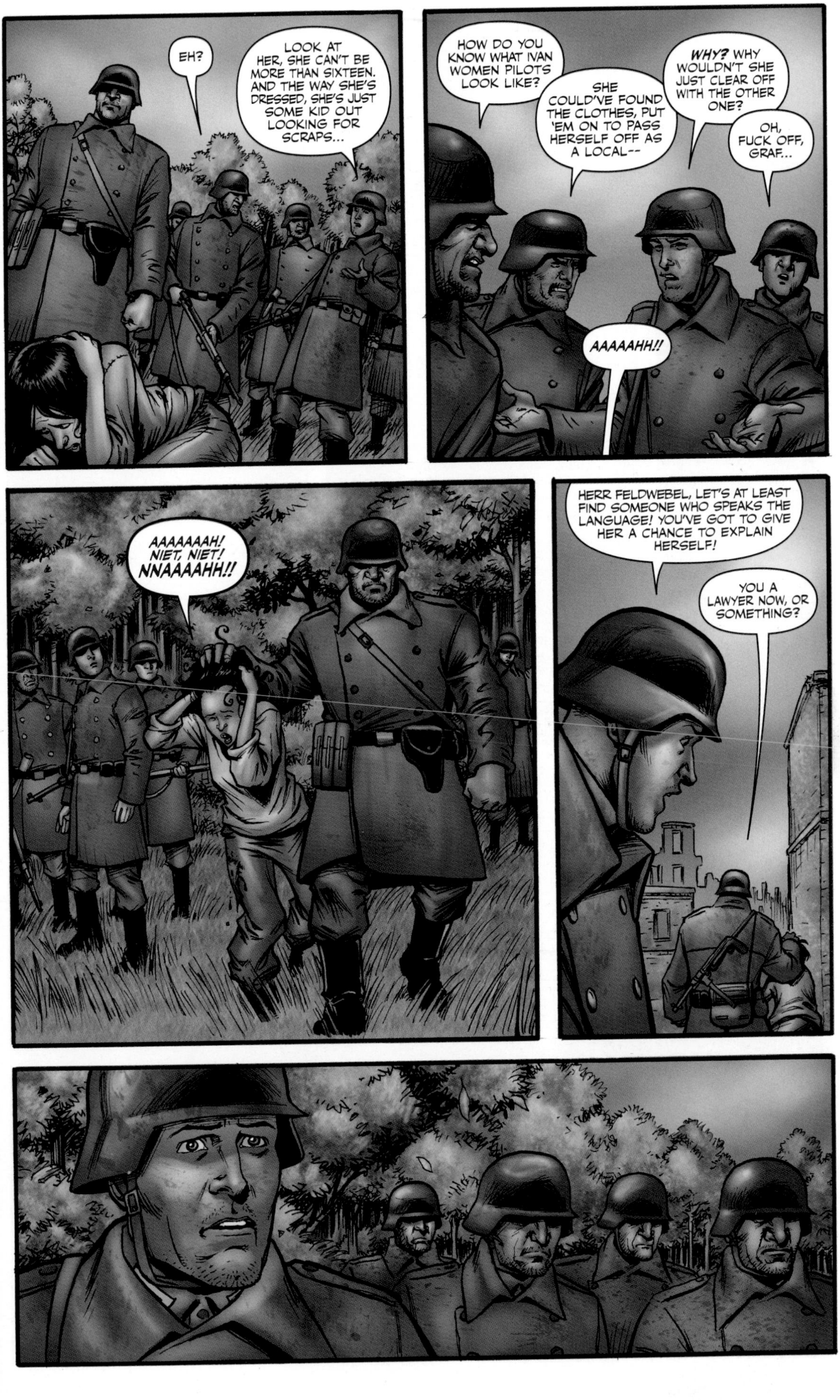
EH?
LOOK AT HER, SHE CAN'T BE MORE THAN SIXTEEN. AND THE WAY SHE'S DRESSED, SHE'S JUST SOME KID OUT LOOKING FOR SCRAPS...
HOW DO YOU KNOW WHAT IVAN WOMEN PILOTS LOOK LIKE?
SHE COULD'VE FOUND THE CLOTHES, PUT 'EM ON TO PASS HERSELF OFF AS A LOCAL--
WHY? WHY WOULDN'T SHE JUST CLEAR OFF WITH THE OTHER ONE?
OH, FUCK OFF, GRAF...
AAAAAHH!!
AAAAAAAH! NIET, NIET! NNAAAAHH!!
HERR FELDWEBEL, LET'S AT LEAST FIND SOMEONE WHO SPEAKS THE LANGUAGE! YOU'VE GOT TO GIVE HER A CHANCE TO EXPLAIN HERSELF!
YOU A LAWYER NOW, OR SOMETHING?

MAN BY MAN, IN THE GLOOM OF AN ABANDONED CELLAR, THE SQUAD DAMNS ITSELF.

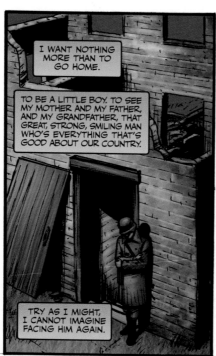

I WANT NOTHING MORE THAN TO GO HOME.

TO BE A LITTLE BOY. TO SEE MY MOTHER AND MY FATHER, AND MY GRANDFATHER, THAT GREAT, STRONG, SMILING MAN WHO'S EVERYTHING THAT'S GOOD ABOUT OUR COUNTRY.

TRY AS I MIGHT, I CANNOT IMAGINE FACING HIM AGAIN.

YOU BETTER GET DOWN THERE.

NO THANKS.

I WOULDN'T FUCK WITH HIM TODAY, GRAF.

NOT IF I WAS YOU.

RIGHT, YOU LITTLE FAIRY: STICK YOUR DICK IN THAT IVAN CUNT AND GET TO WORK.

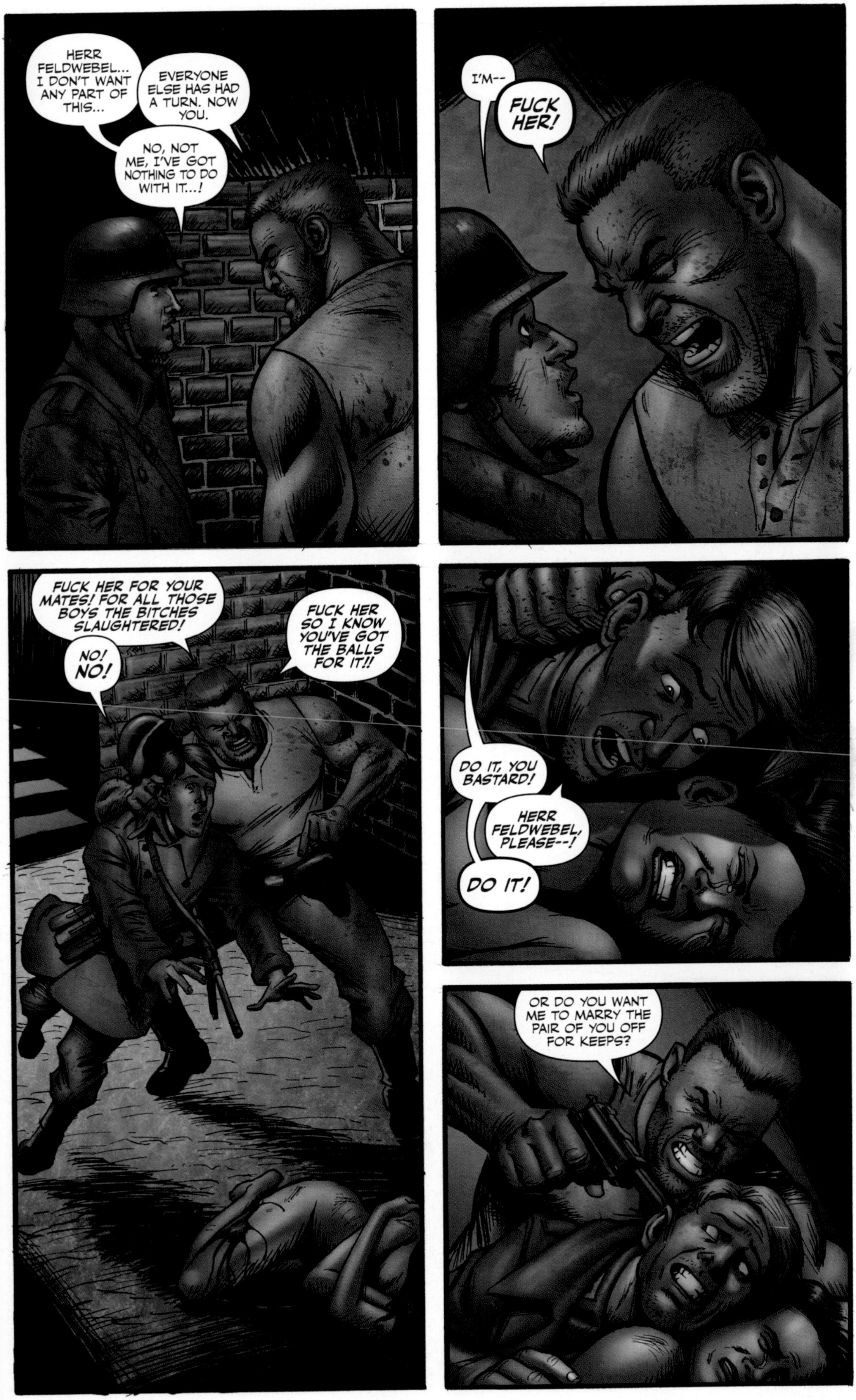
HERR FELDWEBEL... I DON'T WANT ANY PART OF THIS...
EVERYONE ELSE HAS HAD A TURN. NOW YOU.
NO, NOT ME, I'VE GOT NOTHING TO DO WITH IT...!
I'M--
FUCK HER!
FUCK HER FOR YOUR MATES! FOR ALL THOSE BOYS THE BITCHES SLAUGHTERED!
NO! NO!
FUCK HER SO I KNOW YOU'VE GOT THE BALLS FOR IT!!
DO IT, YOU BASTARD!
HERR FELDWEBEL, PLEASE--!
DO IT!
OR DO YOU WANT ME TO MARRY THE PAIR OF YOU OFF FOR KEEPS?

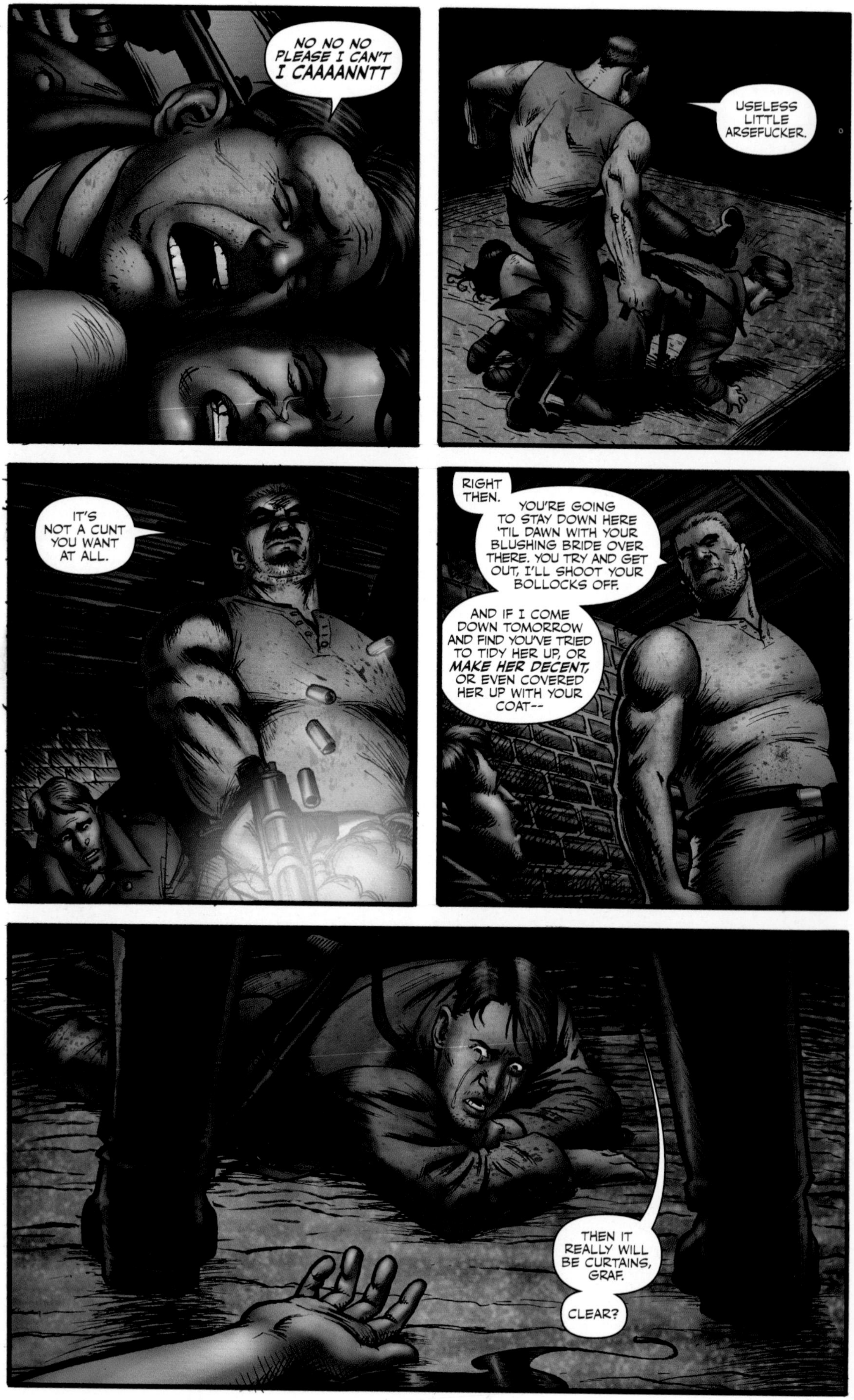

NO NO NO PLEASE I CAN'T I CAAAANNTT
USELESS LITTLE ARSEFUCKER.
IT'S NOT A CUNT YOU WANT AT ALL.
RIGHT THEN.
YOU'RE GOING TO STAY DOWN HERE 'TIL DAWN WITH YOUR BLUSHING BRIDE OVER THERE. YOU TRY AND GET OUT, I'LL SHOOT YOUR BOLLOCKS OFF.
AND IF I COME DOWN TOMORROW AND FIND YOU'VE TRIED TO TIDY HER UP, OR MAKE HER DECENT, OR EVEN COVERED HER UP WITH YOUR COAT--
THEN IT REALLY WILL BE CURTAINS, GRAF.
CLEAR?

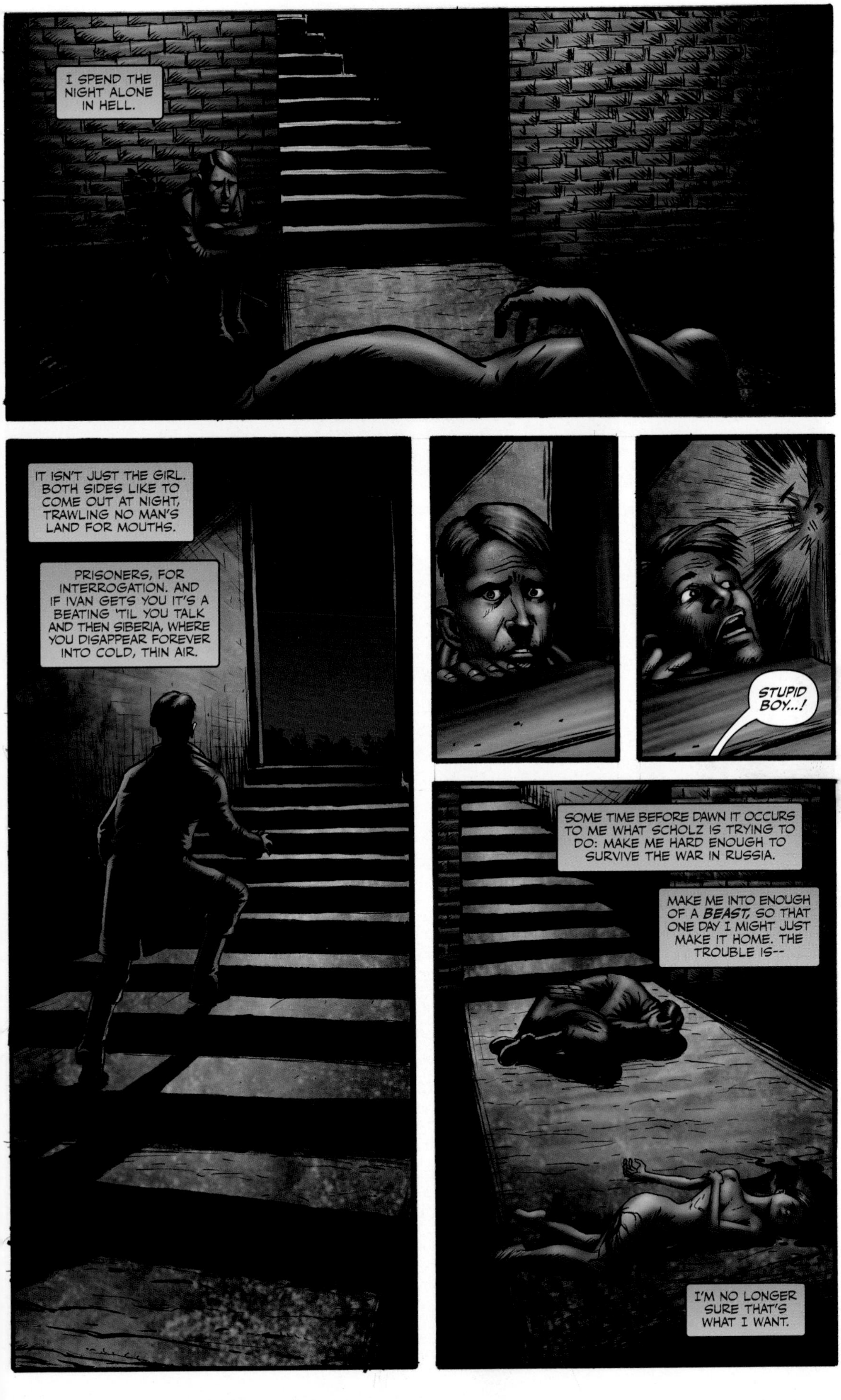
I SPEND THE NIGHT ALONE IN HELL.
IT ISN'T JUST THE GIRL. BOTH SIDES LIKE TO COME OUT AT NIGHT, TRAWLING NO MAN'S LAND FOR MOUTHS.
PRISONERS, FOR INTERROGATION. AND IF IVAN GETS YOU IT'S A BEATING 'TIL YOU TALK AND THEN SIBERIA, WHERE YOU DISAPPEAR FOREVER INTO COLD, THIN AIR.
STUPID BOY...!
SOME TIME BEFORE DAWN IT OCCURS TO ME WHAT SCHOLZ IS TRYING TO DO: MAKE ME HARD ENOUGH TO SURVIVE THE WAR IN RUSSIA.
MAKE ME INTO ENOUGH OF A *BEAST,* SO THAT ONE DAY I MIGHT JUST MAKE IT HOME. THE TROUBLE IS--
I'M NO LONGER SURE THAT'S WHAT I WANT.

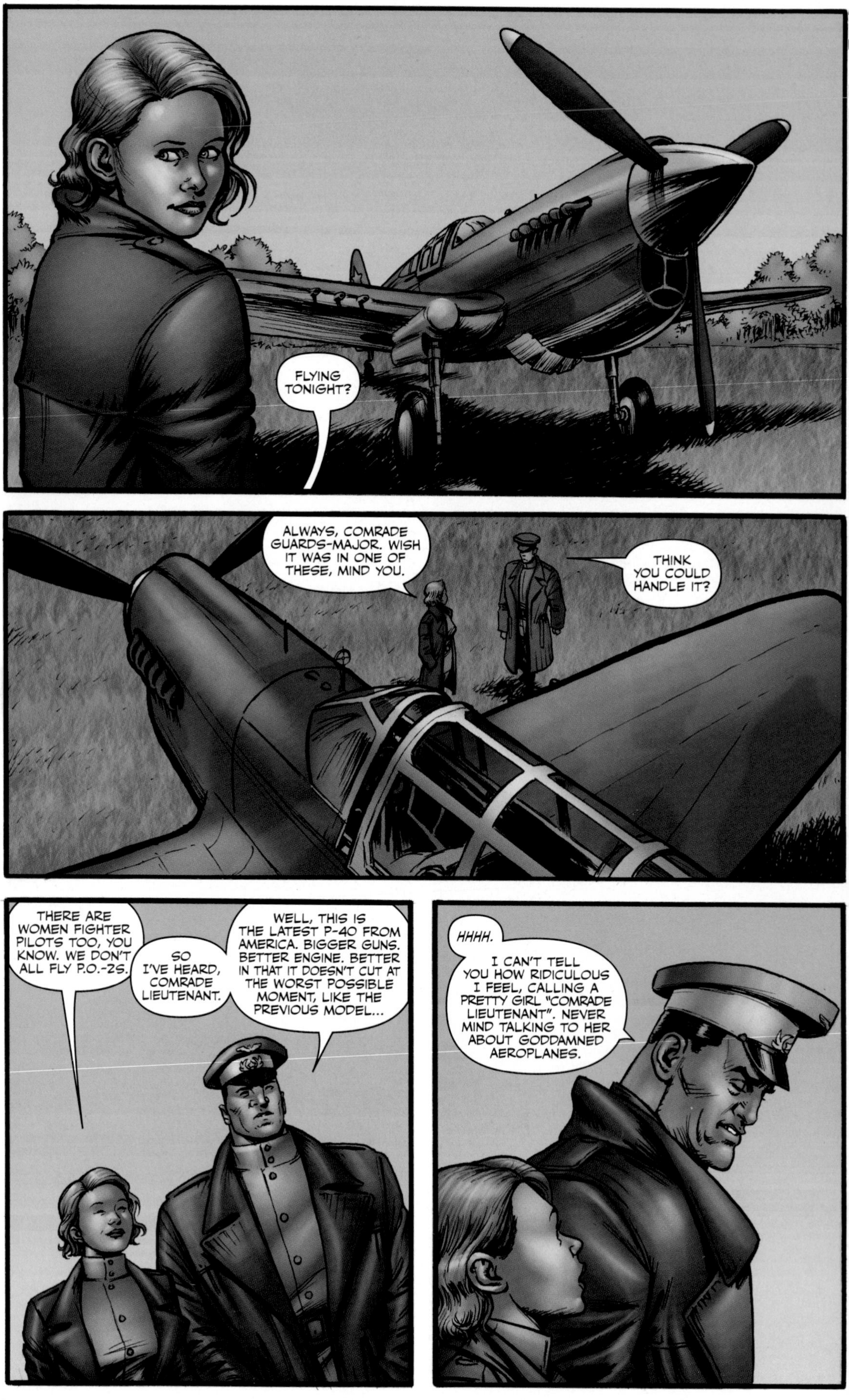
FLYING TONIGHT?
ALWAYS, COMRADE GUARDS-MAJOR. WISH IT WAS IN ONE OF THESE, MIND YOU.
THINK YOU COULD HANDLE IT?
THERE ARE WOMEN FIGHTER PILOTS TOO, YOU KNOW. WE DON'T ALL FLY P.O.-2S.
SO I'VE HEARD, COMRADE LIEUTENANT.
WELL, THIS IS THE LATEST P-40 FROM AMERICA. BIGGER GUNS. BETTER ENGINE. BETTER IN THAT IT DOESN'T CUT AT THE WORST POSSIBLE MOMENT, LIKE THE PREVIOUS MODEL...
HHHH.
I CAN'T TELL YOU HOW RIDICULOUS I FEEL, CALLING A PRETTY GIRL "COMRADE LIEUTENANT". NEVER MIND TALKING TO HER ABOUT GODDAMNED AEROPLANES.

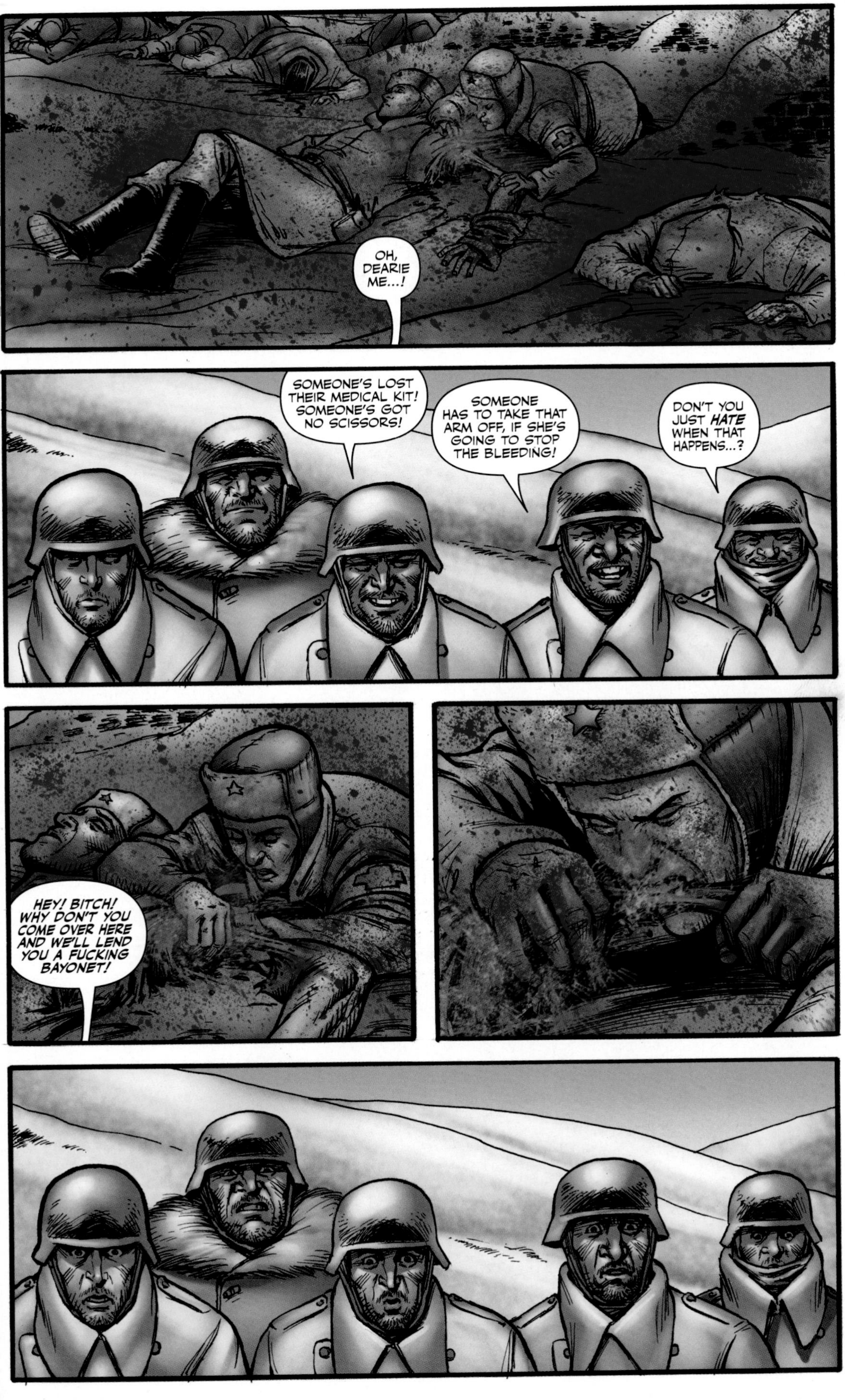
OH, DEARIE ME...!
SOMEONE'S LOST THEIR MEDICAL KIT! SOMEONE'S GOT NO SCISSORS!
SOMEONE HAS TO TAKE THAT ARM OFF, IF SHE'S GOING TO STOP THE BLEEDING!
DON'T YOU JUST HATE WHEN THAT HAPPENS...?
HEY! BITCH! WHY DON'T YOU COME OVER HERE AND WE'LL LEND YOU A FUCKING BAYONET!

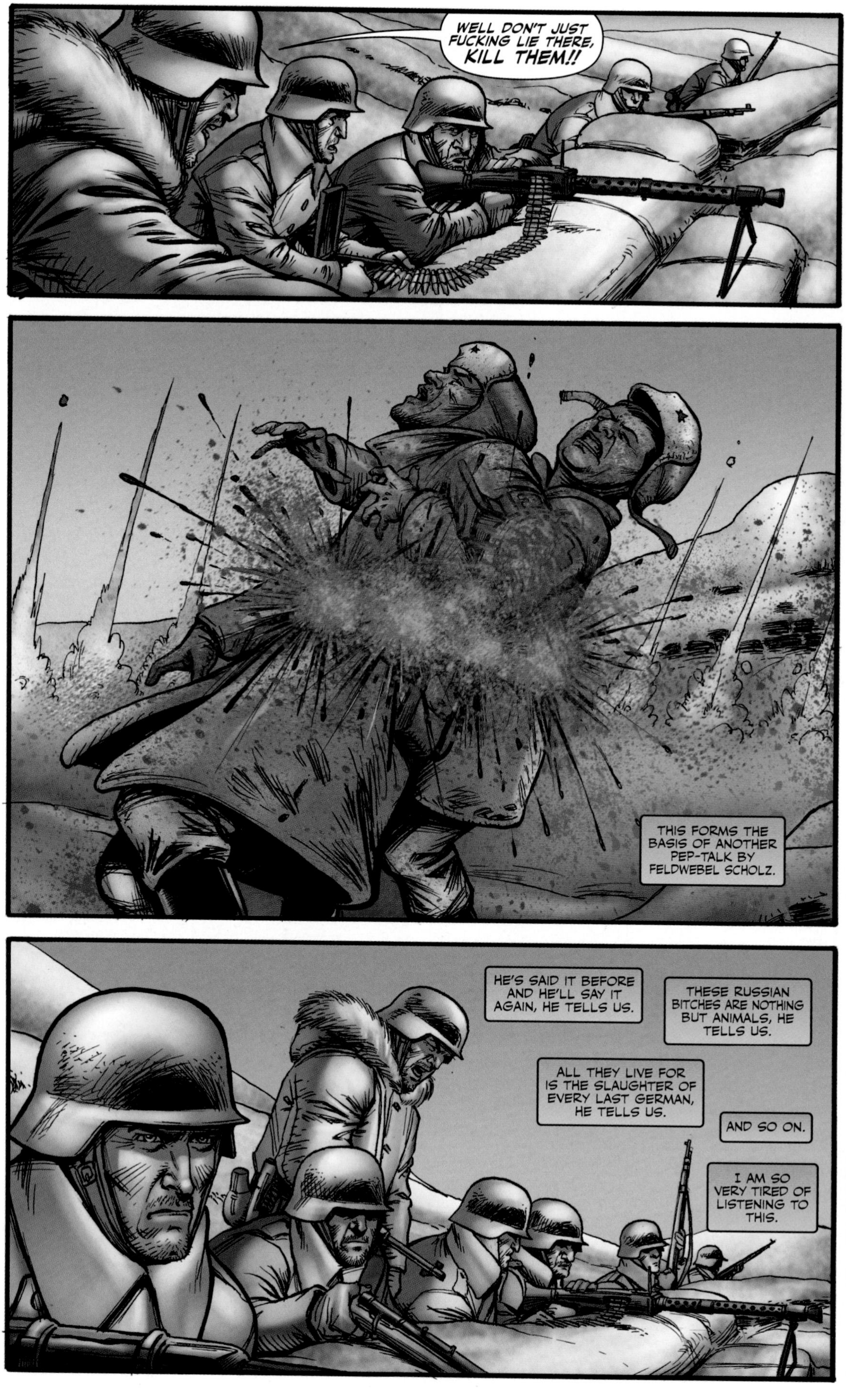
WELL DON'T JUST FUCKING LIE THERE, KILL THEM!!
THIS FORMS THE BASIS OF ANOTHER PEP-TALK BY FELDWEBEL SCHOLZ.
HE'S SAID IT BEFORE AND HE'LL SAY IT AGAIN, HE TELLS US.
THESE RUSSIAN BITCHES ARE NOTHING BUT ANIMALS, HE TELLS US.
ALL THEY LIVE FOR IS THE SLAUGHTER OF EVERY LAST GERMAN, HE TELLS US.
AND SO ON.
I AM SO VERY TIRED OF LISTENING TO THIS.

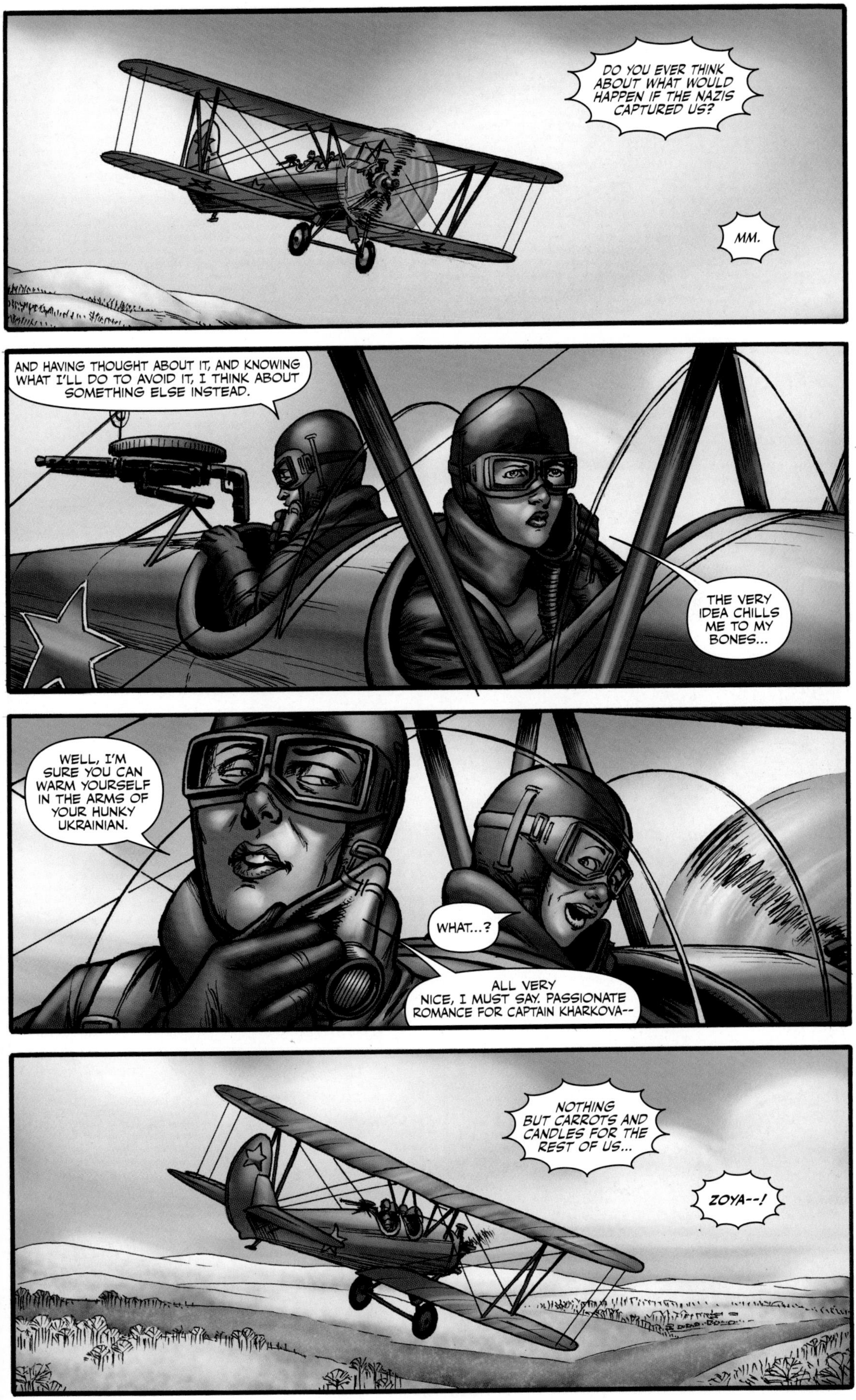
DO YOU EVER THINK ABOUT WHAT WOULD HAPPEN IF THE NAZIS CAPTURED US?
MM.
AND HAVING THOUGHT ABOUT IT, AND KNOWING WHAT I'LL DO TO AVOID IT, I THINK ABOUT SOMETHING ELSE INSTEAD.
THE VERY IDEA CHILLS ME TO MY BONES...
WELL, I'M SURE YOU CAN WARM YOURSELF IN THE ARMS OF YOUR HUNKY UKRAINIAN.
WHAT...?
ALL VERY NICE, I MUST SAY. PASSIONATE ROMANCE FOR CAPTAIN KHARKOVA--
NOTHING BUT CARROTS AND CANDLES FOR THE REST OF US...
ZOYA--!

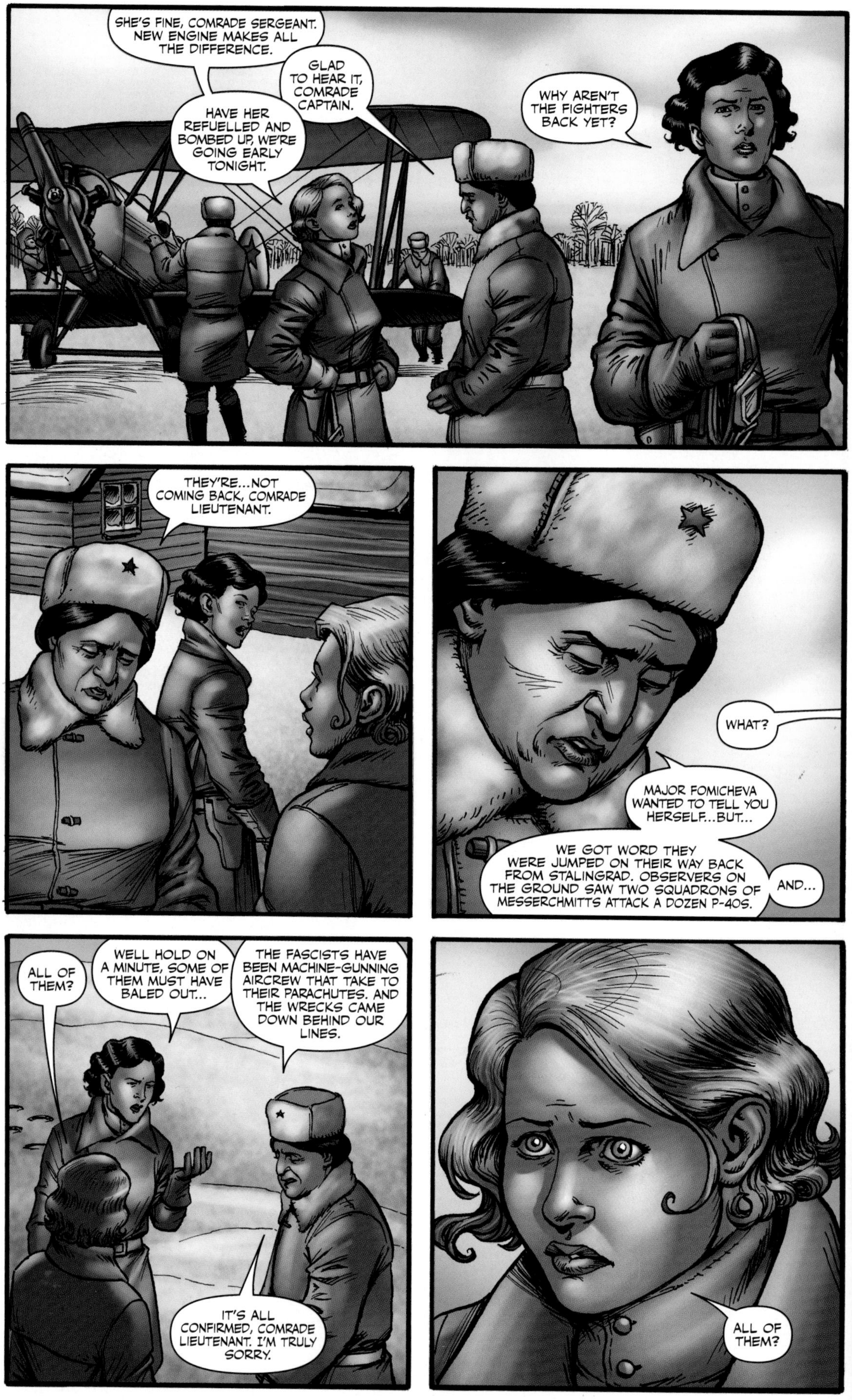
SHE'S FINE, COMRADE SERGEANT. NEW ENGINE MAKES ALL THE DIFFERENCE.
HAVE HER REFUELLED AND BOMBED UP, WE'RE GOING EARLY TONIGHT.
GLAD TO HEAR IT, COMRADE CAPTAIN.
WHY AREN'T THE FIGHTERS BACK YET?
THEY'RE...NOT COMING BACK, COMRADE LIEUTENANT.
WHAT?
MAJOR FOMICHEVA WANTED TO TELL YOU HERSELF...BUT...
WE GOT WORD THEY WERE JUMPED ON THEIR WAY BACK FROM STALINGRAD. OBSERVERS ON THE GROUND SAW TWO SQUADRONS OF MESSERCHMITTS ATTACK A DOZEN P-40S.
AND...
ALL OF THEM?
WELL HOLD ON A MINUTE, SOME OF THEM MUST HAVE BALED OUT...
THE FASCISTS HAVE BEEN MACHINE-GUNNING AIRCREW THAT TAKE TO THEIR PARACHUTES. AND THE WRECKS CAME DOWN BEHIND OUR LINES.
IT'S ALL CONFIRMED, COMRADE LIEUTENANT. I'M TRULY SORRY.
ALL OF THEM?

Sketches and designs by Russ Braun

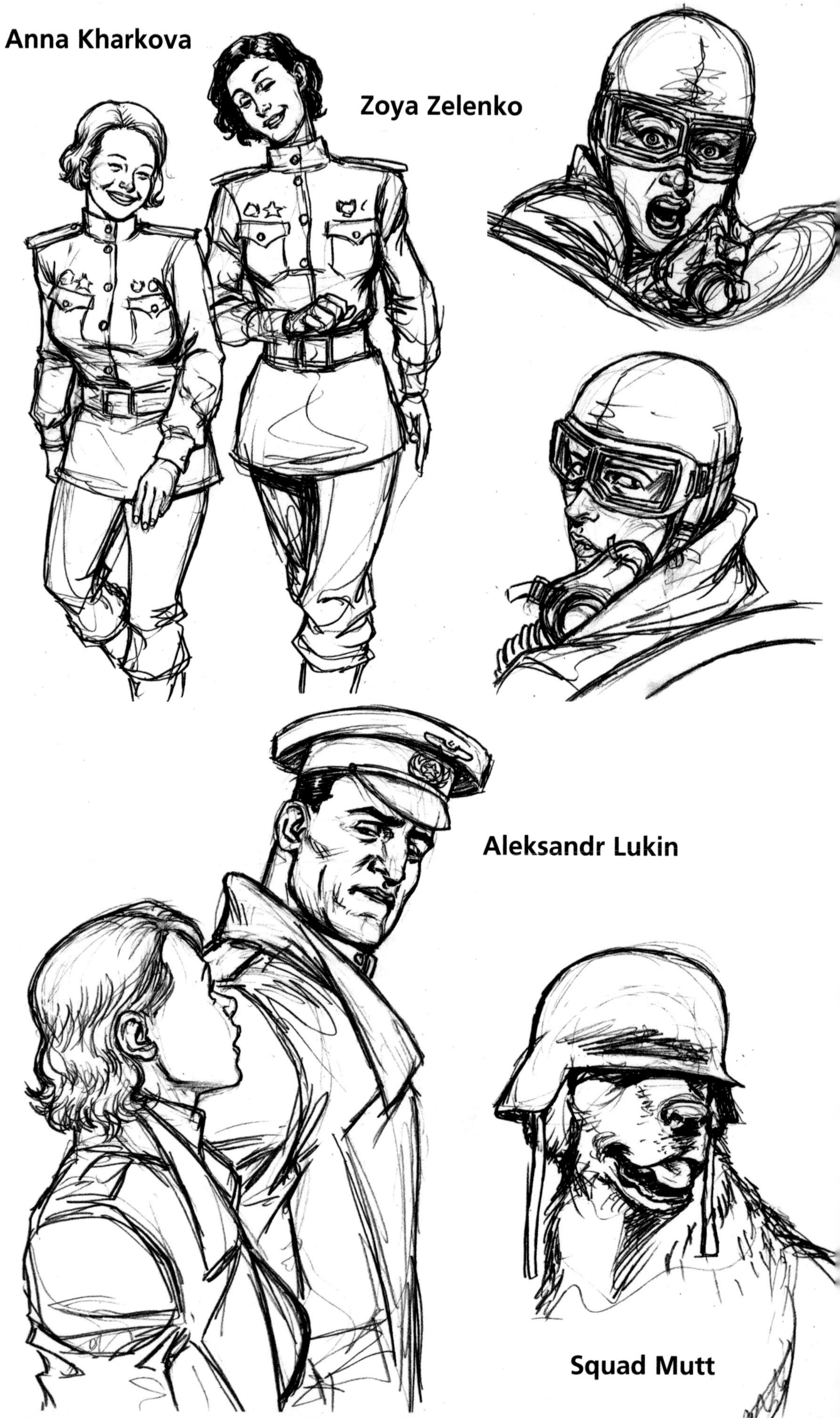
Anna Kharkova
Zoya Zelenko
Aleksandr Lukin
Squad Mutt

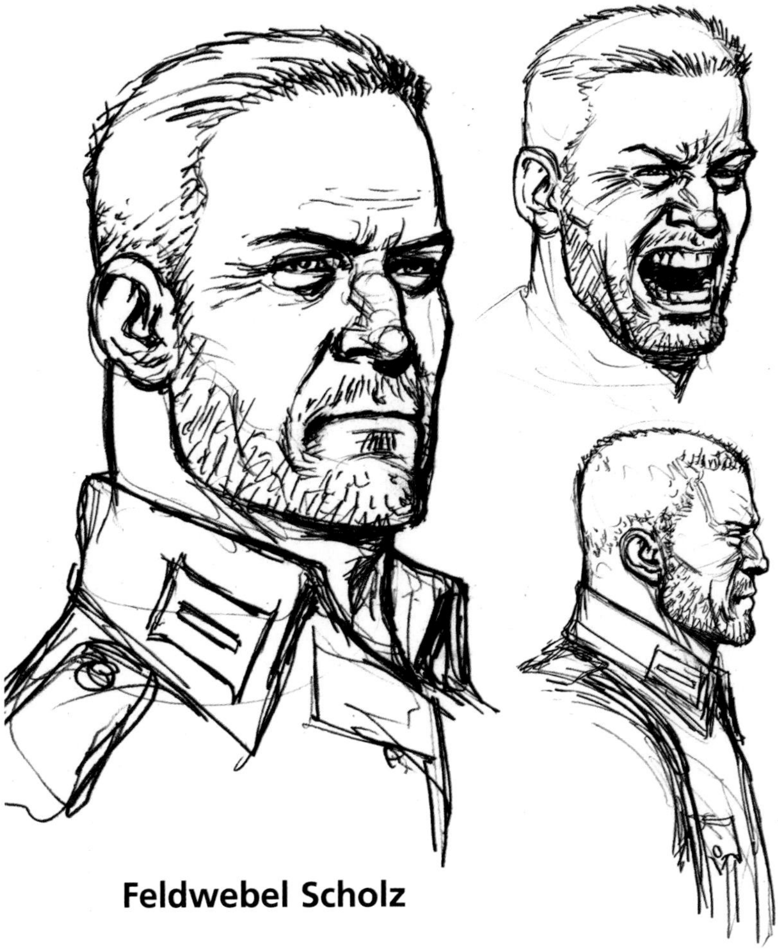

Feldwebel Scholz

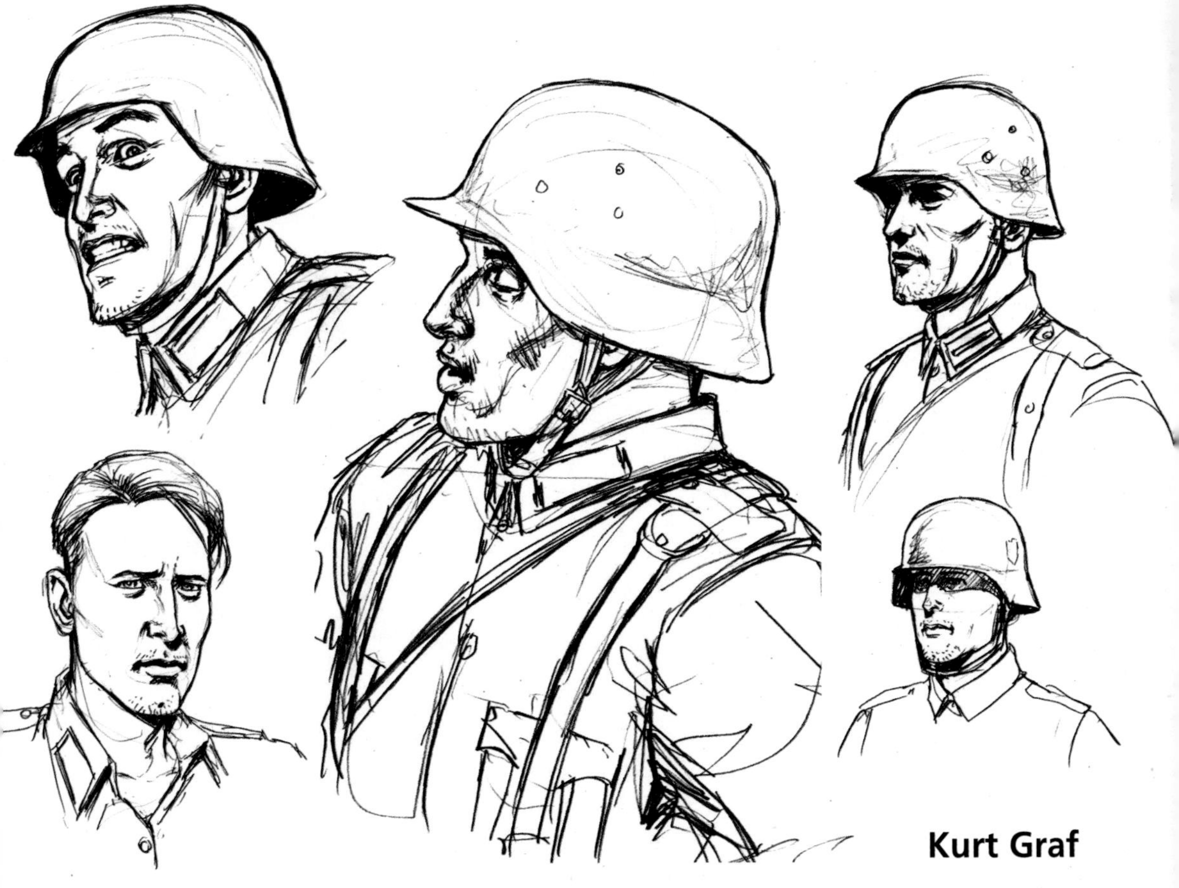

Kurt Graf

Gloomy Fozo

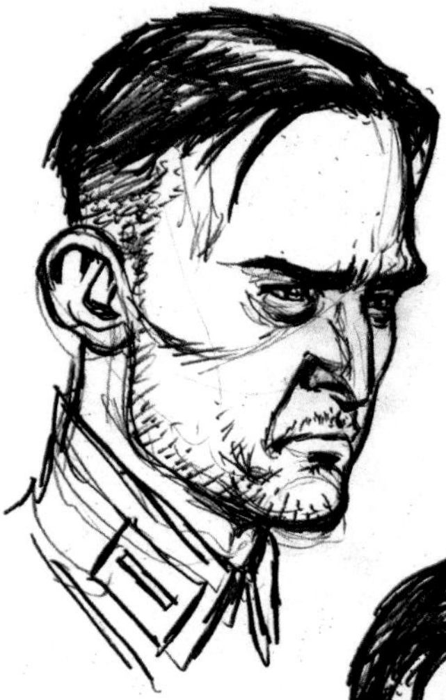

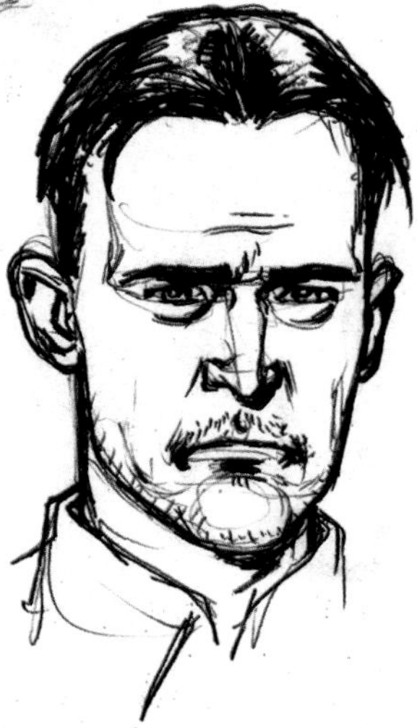

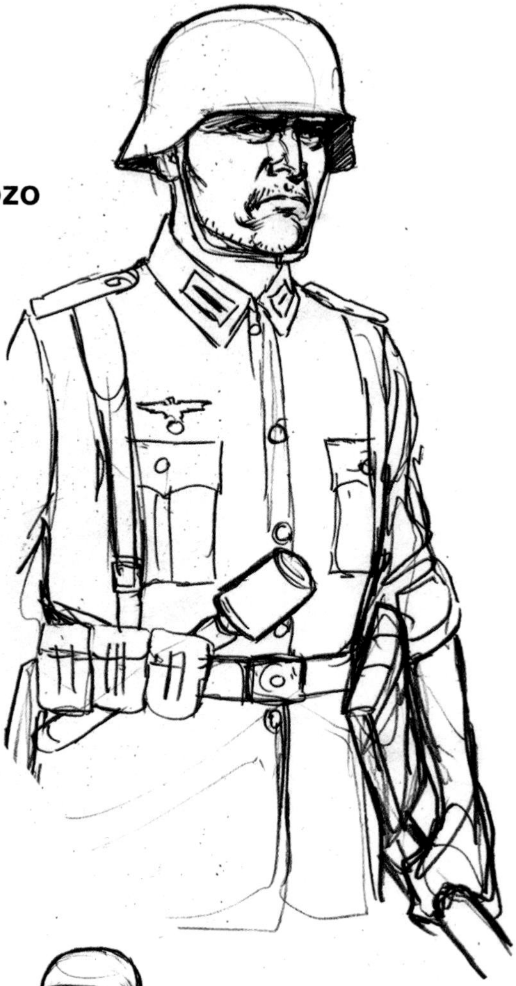

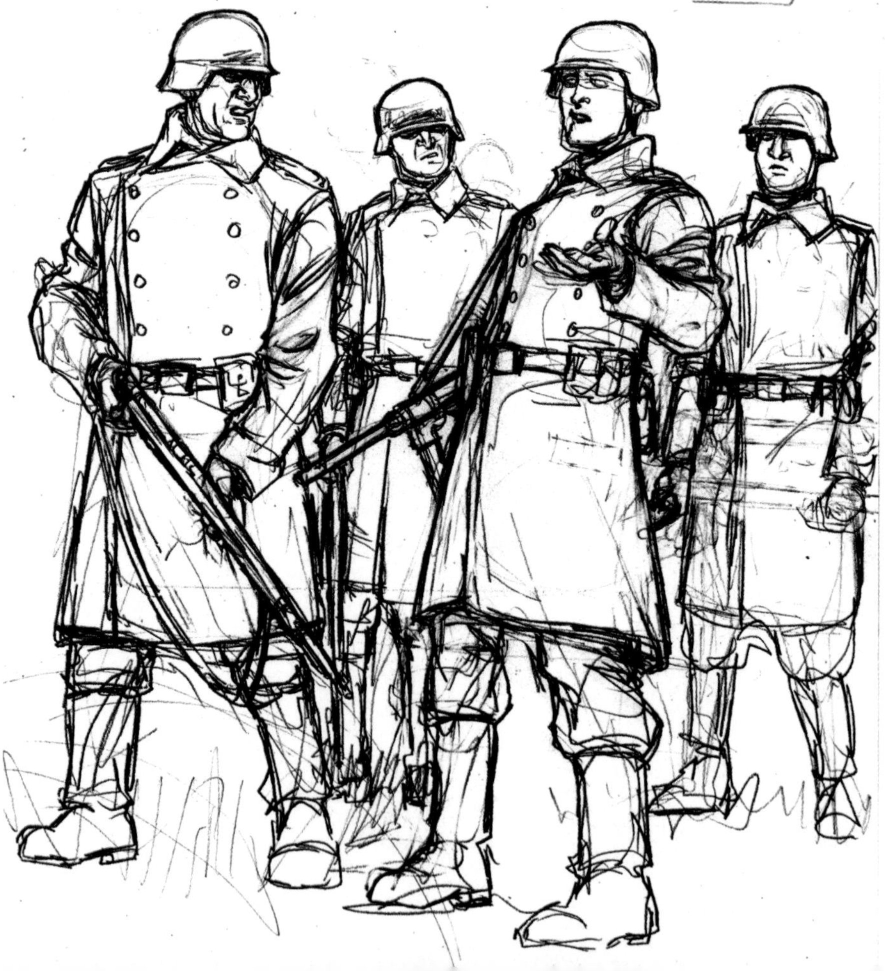